RODEO AUSTIN

Rodeo
AUSTIN

BLUE RIBBONS, BUCKIN' BRONCS & BIG DREAMS

LIZ CARMACK

Foreword by Bucky Lamb

The Story of the
Star of Texas Fair and Rodeo

TEXAS A&M UNIVERSITY PRESS • COLLEGE STATION

This paper meets the requirements
of ANSI/NISO Z39.48-1992
(Permanence of Paper).
Binding materials have been chosen for durability.

LIBRARY OF CONGRESS
CATALOGING-IN-PUBLICATION DATA

Carmack, Liz.
    Rodeo Austin : blue ribbons, buckin' broncs, and big
dreams : the story of the Star of Texas Fair and Rodeo / Liz
Carmack ; foreword by Bucky Lamb.—1st ed.
        p. cm.
    Includes bibliographical references and index.
    ISBN 978-1-60344-568-9 (book/hardcover (printed case) :
alk. paper)
    ISBN 978-1-60344-589-4 (ebook format/ebook—c)
1. Star of Texas Fair and Rodeo—History—20th century.
2. Star of Texas Fair and Rodeo—History—21st century.
3. Livestock exhibitions—Texas—Austin—History—20th century.
4. Livestock exhibitions—Texas—Austin—History—21st century.
5. Rodeos —Texas—Austin—History—20th century.
6. Rodeos—Texas—Austin—History—21st century.   7. Star
of Texas Fair and Rodeo—Endowments.   8. Star of Texas
Fair and Rodeo—Awards.   9. Youth—Scholarships, fellow-
ships, etc.—Texas—Austin.   10. Austin (Tex.)—Social life and
customs—20th century.   11. Austin (Tex.)—Social life and
customs—21st century.   I. Title.
    SF117.65.T42C37   2012
    791.8'40976431—dc23
    2011024061

CONTENTS

RODEO AUSTIN

The Star of Texas Fair and Rodeo is one of the fastest-growing charities of its kind in the nation. The Austin organization awards more than $400,000 annually in college scholarships to deserving students throughout the state. It funnels another more than $1.5 million each year to support over 14,500 youth participating in the charity's livestock show, Western art show, youth auction, and other educational events.

Its 15-night Rodeo Austin (a ProRodeo sanctioned by the Professional Rodeo Cowboys Association, or PRCA), the live concerts featuring chart-topping musical acts, and its bustling fairgrounds are among the action-packed March attractions for which the organization is primarily known. These events, plus year-round fund-raising efforts by more than 1,500 volunteers and support from local and national sponsors, have raised more than $30 million for youth during the past 30 years.

Its dual mission, "Promoting Youth Education—Preserving Western Heritage," was formalized in 2000. But these goals have been a unifying thread since the Austin Chamber of Commerce began planning Austin's first livestock show, the tiny predecessor of today's statewide event. Promoting education (of both youth *and* adults) was the main impetus that prompted the chamber to stage the first show. These boosters of the area's economy saw a need to develop the local livestock market and hoped to teach area farming families how to properly raise and feed calves.

In 1938, the chamber first discussed plans to hold a livestock show in Austin. Then in 1940, working closely with the Travis County Agricultural Extension Service agent, the chamber staged Austin's first *Baby Beef Show*. The small event was held on the temporary State Capitol grounds at Eleventh Street and Congress Avenue, across the street from the State Capitol. Since then, the annual livestock show's thousands

Proceeds from Rodeo Austin ticket sales help fund college scholarships and other educational programs for youth. (Courtesy Star of Texas Fair and Rodeo)

A participant in the 1957 Austin Livestock Show holds her sheep during judging. (Russell Lee Collection, di_07031, The Dolph Briscoe Center for American History, The University of Texas at Austin)

Rodeo Austin
March 21, 2010 ✩ 3:00 PM
ProRodeo & Live Entertainment
Star of Texas Fair & Rodeo
Travis County Expo Center

of entrants have learned best practices for raising their animals and have garnered valuable hands-on experience, teaching them how to achieve their goals through hard work and responsibility.

The organization took on a larger commitment to education in 1981 when it began awarding college scholarships to deserving youth who participated in its livestock show. Today show participation is not necessary to become a scholarship winner. In fact, many of the more than 40 students receiving the $2,500 to $16,000 scholarships each year have never even attended a livestock show or seen a rodeo.

These young Texans represent a growing populace who can't tell the difference between a steer and a heifer and who have no clue what a lariat is or what a cutting horse does. On March 16, 1940, when the first group gathered to show 16 calves in downtown Austin, it was probably even then an unusual site for city slickers in a community of almost 88,000. But there were more than 2,600 farms in Travis County at that time, so Austin still had strong ties to agriculture. Those ties were so significant that the Austin chamber had its own Agricultural Bureau to help develop this part of the economy.

By contrast today, most Travis County and Texas citizens live in urban areas and have little daily contact with farming and ranching and the Western culture and traditions upon which the state was founded. This fact gives the second part of the charity's mission, "Preserving Western Heritage," growing importance in the twenty-first century. The more than 7,000 schoolchildren who tour the Travis County Exposition Center fairgrounds each year can learn where their milk comes from, witness a sheep dog trial, or watch other youngsters prep their calves, hogs, and goats as they head to the show ring. Even Rodeo Austin patrons learn about the roots of what has become a pro sport, as velvet-voiced announcers detail the skills cowboys have long needed to succeed at calf roping or describe how the rodeo saddle bronc riding competition developed from cowboys breaking wild horses.

Throughout its history, the livestock show has survived a continuous evolution of its sponsors, donors, and leaders. It has expanded from a tiny Travis County show to one that welcomes 4-H and FFA (formerly Future Farmers of America) youth from across the state. And its rodeo, which had humble 1950s beginnings in the cramped City Coliseum, is now a ProRodeo featuring world-champion cowboys and cowgirls.

Over the years, the group has weathered controversies, gone through periods of organizational upheaval, reaped gains during Austin's flush times, and endured financial setbacks when the economy was not so rosy. In the early 1980s, it left the chamber's sponsorship and officially became a nonprofit charity. During that same decade it relied upon an unprecedented level of support from its volunteers and Austin area businesses to construct a new, larger facility. From its new home at the Travis County Exposition Center, it has expanded its programs and attractions and increased its contributions to youth each year.

Rodeo Austin is the world's fifth-largest indoor, regular season ProRodeo. (Courtesy Star of Texas Fair and Rodeo)

DATE: MARCH 19, 2011
#AD3-1911-13

Jumping boots first into the twenty-first century, it has exploited high-tech tools, the Internet, and social media to support its mission by reaching a larger audience. Leaders also rely upon long-range planning to stay ahead of trends in the rodeo and fair industry and to better understand their audience and how best to engage them.

A look back at the show's more than seven-decade history reveals unexpected details about these events and paints a telling portrait of the charity's close relationship with the Austin community. Today, the well-worn Expo Center's facilities are being strained to the breaking point as the fair draws 300,000 visitors annually, and the charity's board faces difficult decisions about its future. As the saying goes, "History repeats itself." Four times during its

The Travis County Exposition Center in northeast Austin has been home to the Star of Texas Fair and Rodeo since 1984. (Courtesy Star of Texas Fair and Rodeo)

history, the first in 1942, the show outgrew its home and had to seek a larger venue. The future of the Star of Texas Fair and Rodeo will once again depend upon how its leaders deal with this challenge, one brought on by its own success.

Farming and ranching were important parts of the Austin area economy in the 1930s. Statistics from the time reveal why: Travis County had more than 3,000 farms in 1935. Eighty-two percent of the area land was either growing crops such as cotton, grains, potatoes, or peaches or was plowable pasture. In 1935, the U.S. Census of Agriculture reported there were 17,624 cows and heifers over the age of two, 11,634 dairy cows, 19,766 sheep and lambs, 20,882 goats and kids, 151,199 chickens, and 6,758 turkeys in Travis County.

The Austin Chamber of Commerce's *General Facts and Statistical Review of Austin, Texas, 1939* (which served as both a promotional piece touting the city as a wonderful place to live and a statistical snapshot of the community) described the land to the city's

east as home to "well-kept farms, producing an abundance of dairy products and garden products, as well as large crops of cotton, corn, hay and other feed crops . . . an important and stabilizing force in the economic life of the community."

By the late 1930s, Austin had emerged from the Great Depression with a local economy fueled not only by area agricultural production but also by the University of Texas, state government agencies, and a manufacturing base that produced everything from bed springs, concrete pipe, and structural steel to flavoring extracts, cigars, and potato chips.

It is telling, though, that the chamber gave the "Agriculture" and "Livestock" sections of its statistical review equal weight alongside the sections detailing the city's educational resources, churches, industries, and climate. To the chamber, developing the practice of agriculture in Travis and its adjacent counties (then called the Austin Trade Area) was just as important as recruiting a new manufacturing plant to the city. Thus, the chamber formed an Agricultural Bureau in the 1930s. Its activities were run by a vice president and dozens of volunteers. The bureau worked closely with the Travis County Agricultural Extension Service Agent to boost the agriculture industry and to deal with current issues—from developing new markets for crops and livestock to combating cotton plant root rot.

One concern in 1938 appears to have been a lack of high-quality, locally fattened livestock. An editorial in the March 8, 1938, *Austin American* cites statistics from the Federal Bureau of Agriculture Economics that in January of that year, the state of Texas had more than 7.24 million head of beef:

> So far as mere figures go, it is a fine showing. There are some things wrong with the livestock picture in Texas, however. Entirely too many Texas beeves are sent elsewhere to be fed for market, entirely too few are fed in Texas. That is in spite of the fact that Texas can raise the feed its cattle need. Another unfavorable feature of the figures is in the number of hogs. Texas raises far less pork than it did 20 years ago. It does not raise nearly enough for its own consumption. The livestock industry means much to Texas, but it still means far less than it might mean.

The Austin chamber's 1938 annual report echoed the same concerns: "Experience has demonstrated for many years that it costs about 60 percent as much to produce a pound of weight on livestock in Texas as it does in the extreme northern states." The report noted that growing attention was being focused on livestock production in Travis County.

The area's smaller communities—including Elgin, Buda, and Lockhart—were holding calf, hog, and poultry shows at this time for FFA and 4-H students (primarily boys). And statewide, the Southwestern Exposition and Livestock Show in Fort Worth, founded in 1896, and the Houston Fat Stock Show and Livestock Exhibition, which began in 1931, offered large, well-known events that included rodeos and fairs.

Chamber Plans Austin Baby Beef Show

Around 1938, it appears the seeds for an Austin stock show were planted. The chamber's Agricultural Bureau announced plans in that year's annual report to stage a "fat stock" show in 1939 for fat calves raised by "4-H Club boys and girls in fourteen Central Texas counties." But the idea apparently never came to fruition, and the 1939 annual report, published in January 1940, announced more detailed plans for a show: "The County Agents, knowing for a long time the great value of baby beef production, have the backing of the Agricultural Bureau and in 1940 a fat stock show will be held to encourage the growing of more feed and live stock on the farms of Travis County. The Chamber of Commerce will not only offer cash prizes in this program, but it is also helping find a market for this stock."

During this time, the Travis County Extension Agent's annual summary of the agency's activities was regularly included as part of the chamber's annual report. In his 1939 report, Agent T. H. Royder detailed plans for the 1940 show and sale and encouraged community participation in the auction. "Austin business men, markets, hotels and cafes can assist in building the beef cattle industry and assure themselves better quality meat to sell by their cooperation in this sale."

Calves Judged on Temporary State Capitol Grounds

City residents were no doubt curious the morning of Wednesday, March 6, 1940, when men, boys, and their calves began to gather in the heart of downtown across the street from the Texas State Capitol. According to newspaper and chamber reports, Austin's first Baby Beef Show and sale, scheduled from 2:00 to 5:00 P.M., was held at the temporary State Capitol grounds on the southwest corner of Eleventh Street and Congress Avenue. The event was a joint effort by the chamber's Agricultural Bureau and Agent Royder. The oddity reportedly attracted an audience of 5,000 to 6,000 in a community of about 88,000.

Competitors were divided into two groups: men and boys who were members of 4-H clubs in Travis County. Each group's entries were split into classes according to animal weight. In the boys' group, the 755-pound grand champion calf, owned by Vernon Carson of Creed-

moor, sold for 27.5 cents per pound to Harry Akin of Night Hawk Restaurants. Raymond Hees of Richland won reserve champion. The Driskill Hotel purchased Hees's 1,040-pound animal for 15 cents per pound. The chamber distributed ribbons to the winners, as well as $18 in prize money to Carson and $8 to Hees. Sixteen boys in all entered the event. The men's competition apparently had four entries, with Calvin Hughes taking first place in the heavy class and H. E. Wattinger winning the light class, with a calf "raised and fed out by Joe Davis, Jr., a young farm boy on the Wattinger place."

D. S. Buchanan headed up the judging, and Joe McBride served as auctioneer for the sale. Walter Gunn, manager of the Austin Stock Yards, also assisted. The chamber committee members directing the event were George C. Quinn (chairman), a manager with South Texas Cotton Oil Co.; Charles Schneider, a manager with Swift & Co.; E. R. L. Wroe, president of American National Bank; Reece Meador, president of Home Mix Feed Co.; Gordon B. Rogers, manager of Armour & Co.; Agent Royder; Akin; D. S. Buchanan; Ira E. Stacy, of Stacy's Meat Products; Steve Heffington, Travis County tax assessor and collector; Gunn; and Irwin W. Popham, Travis County superintendent of schools.

Show Participation Grows Quickly

The size of the show more than doubled in 1941, with the chamber reporting conflicting tallies (in separate publications) of 40 entries

The grand champion banner at the first Austin Baby Beef Show could have resembled this re-creation. (Courtesy Star of Texas Fair and Rodeo)

and 51 entries by 4-H and FFA boys. Vernon Carson and Raymond Hees repeated their wins from the previous year. Carson's 945-pound calf won grand champion and was auctioned for $0.45 per pound to Austin & Barrow supermarket for $425.25. The grocery store also purchased 11 additional calves during the show. Hees sold his reserve champion calf for $0.16 per pound to Charles Balagia of Balagia Produce and Market.

In 1942, the growing event was moved to the Municipal Market House at the intersection of East Avenue (which is now Interstate Highway 35) and Seventh Street. The chamber and the county agricultural agent referred to the event by slightly different names that year—the *Travis County Club Boys' Calf Show* and the *Travis County Boys' Livestock Show*, respectively. It had grown enough that it now took two days to accommodate the show's expanded classes for Angus and Herefords, a few hogs, and the animal auction. The chamber reported that 70 calves (the extension agent reported 71) sold for an average price of $0.16 per pound; the Aberdeen Angus calf shown by Ted Lehman of Pilot Knob won grand champion. The 250-pound grand champion Hampshire hog, shown by Oswald Cumby of Manor, sold for $0.51 per pound. The *Statesman* reported that it was the highest price ever paid for a hog on the Austin market.

"They had the show down where the [Austin] police station is now. There was no security. You could walk anywhere you wanted to," said Marvin Hamann, who was a Richland 4-H Club member at the time. "The second day I came down there, and my calf was grazing on that [Waller] creek." Hamann was able to collect his calf in time for the auction. He won third place in the showmanship contest during the 1942 show and today remembers his treasured prize—"a genuine leather belt" from Grove Drug on East Sixth Street.

According to the chamber, one individual and four area businesses—R. E. Janes; Armour & Co.; J. C. Penney Co.; Sears, Roebuck Co.; and Kash-Karry Stores—provided "special prizes" to the winners to supplement cash and ribbons received from the chamber. This is the first mention of prizes being provided by sources other than the chamber.

The Austin Chamber of Commerce staged the show at the Municipal Market House from 1942 to 1946. (Courtesy Austin Chamber of Commerce)

Austin Municipal Abattoir. (PICA 00609, Austin History Center, Austin Public Library)

The City of Austin operated the Austin Municipal Abattoir, at the intersection of East Fifth Street and Pleasant Valley Road, and processed the auctioned animals at no charge during the show's early years. The slaughterhouse opened in 1931 and closed in 1969.

Volunteer support to ensure the event's success grew in 1943, in part because of the country's growing involvement in World War II and its effect on chamber staffing. That year, the chamber noted that its agricultural secretary, Jim Boswell, was away serving with the military in New Guinea, a fact that made it "necessary to rely almost entirely on volunteer help in this agricultural work. Eight volunteer sub-committees handled—most ably—the work for the Beef and Hog Show." More than 80 people worked on the show under the leadership of Joe C. Carrington, general chairman.

As early as 1944, both boys *and* girls were involved in the show. Carolyn Voelker Sandlin's family farmed land between Elgin and Manor, and she competed with calves at the Austin

EARLY EDUCATION DEVELOPS LOCAL LIVESTOCK MARKET

Education was an important part of Austin's first livestock show, and head judge D. S. Buchanan reviewed the aspects of a good calf with each contestant. For the attending crowd, he compared a well-fed calf to one that had been fed only pasture grass. "Buchanan pointed out why the well fed calf was superior to a butcher, and in the auction that followed the better type calf brought twice as much as the other," reported the *Austin Statesman* on March 7, 1940.

The boys competing also got a taste of how the free-enterprise system worked through their efforts and learned how to track expenses and what a profit was. The top winners' calves were sold at prices that were much higher than the going market rate of $0.10 per pound, Royder reported. But he noted other participants managed to turn a profit even at the going rate by feeding their stock "home-grown grain and feed stuff." In one example, Wilfred Fuchs of Richland netted $32.23. The boy's total expenses were $58.27, and his 905-pound calf brought $90.50 at the sale. Fuchs also was awarded $4.00 for his fourth-place finish in the heavyweight class.

In 1942, Travis County Agricultural Extension Agent K. D. Willingham reported that the calf-feeding demonstrations (provided through the Baby Beef shows and the 4-H program) were causing "neighboring farmers to feed their calves and even buy calves to feed. There are now probably a thousand or more herd [sic] of feeder yearlings and calves in

the feed lots of this county." (Willingham probably meant to write "a thousand or more head" of feeder yearlings.)

The chamber tooted its own horn in its 1943 annual report by illustrating how the nascent show and sale and the associated efforts to educate youth and the public about livestock breeding and feeding had changed the marketplace:

Five years ago calves for boys [4-H and FFA] clubs were purchased from surrounding cattle counties. An educational program has caused many of the boys' daddies to become beef cattle producers and this year practically all calves were purchased localy [sic], indicating additional income to farm groups of approximately $75,000. . . . We are eating meat today in Austin because of the foresight of the Agricultural Committee and a vigorous City Council.

Willingham detailed further results from this effort by noting in his annual report that "we now have several breeders of registered beef cattle in Travis County, including two 4-H club boys. . . . The club boys of Travis County are now feeding twice as many calves and hogs as they did in 1942."

By 1945, the U.S. Government Agricultural Census reported that the value of livestock and livestock products in Travis County totaled $1.17 million.

Boys who participated in the 1943 livestock show hold what could be certificates or checks from the auction. (Courtesy Austin Chamber of Commerce)

Ted Lehman's steer won grand champion during the 1943 show. A Pilot Knob resident and member of the Creedmoor 4-H Club, Lehman sold his Hereford to the Chicken Shack for $0.57 per pound at the auction. (Courtesy Austin Chamber of Commerce)

Harvey Jacobson of Round Rock, center, exhibited the grand champion hog at the 1943 show. The Union Stock Yards purchased it at auction for $0.30 per pound. (Courtesy Austin Chamber of Commerce)

A crowd at the Municipal Market House watches as a livestock judge (center) sizes up cattle during the 1943 show. (Courtesy Austin Chamber of Commerce)

Fifteen-year-old Carolyn Voelker poses with her reserve grand champion steer at the 1945 Austin Livestock Show. The 876-pound calf was purchased by Leslie's Chicken Shack for $0.50 per pound. (Courtesy Carolyn Voelker Sandlin)

show for three years during the 1940s under the tutelage of longtime Elgin High School agricultural teacher J. Z. Hattox. She and five other girls exhibited calves in 1945, and her calf won reserve champion. A retired teacher today, Sandlin recalled the judging that year. "It was very close between the grand champion and my calf," she said. The grand champion winner Joe Ed Johnson and she made an exciting trip to Austin after their wins to celebrate at a chamber dinner. Sandlin put her earnings from the sale of her winning calf toward the cost of her college education.

Youth stepped up to help lead the event in 1945. Chairmen and vice-chairmen of the 11

chamber committees responsible for the show apparently felt that the boys and girls involved would develop consistent interest in it if they took some of the responsibility for its staging, under the guidance of the chamber. The chamber reported that on December 9, 1944, county agent K. D. Willingham called a special meeting to organize the next show, now named the *Travis County Junior Livestock Show.* The following youth officers were elected during the meeting: president, Elwood Nelson, Elroy; vice-president, Leo Luedtke, Pflugerville; secretary, Lanelle Riedel, Turnerville; treasurer, Miles Mehner, Manor. At this meeting their constitution and bylaws were formulated, and the rules and regulations for the 1945 Livestock Show were completed.

By the mid-1940s, the Austin community's involvement and support for the event had widened. In 1944, the Bergstrom Air Field Band performed during the evening program prior to the awards presentation. A growing list of individuals and businesses made in-kind and cash donations during the 1940s to help the chamber cover its costs for the show, and a growing list of buyers paid top dollar at the sale—support that would continue to grow throughout the decades to come.

City Coliseum Becomes New Home

The Municipal Market House barely held the growing event, which was adding new animal classes and staging the show in conjunction with others. In 1945, the swine entries alone taxed the pens to capacity. The first exhibition of the Travis County Registered Hereford Breeders Association show was held in conjunction with the Austin show in 1945, as were shows for students from the Texas School for the Deaf and the Austin State School. In 1946, capons and lambs were part of the Travis County Junior Livestock Show, and in 1947, dairy heifers were exhibited.

Show leaders had formed a Coliseum-Auditorium Committee in 1945 to identify a new venue that could host the livestock show and other community events. Travis County dairyman Herman Heep chaired the group, which included Max Starcke, Raymond Brooks,

1945 Travis County Junior Livestock Show Program

Thursday, February 22

10:00 a.m.—All Livestock Entries—Beef, Lambs, and Hogs—Entered and in Place

11:00 a.m.—Sifting of Calves and Hogs by Sifting Committee

11:00 a.m.—Judging of Hereford Breeding Cattle

12:30 p.m.—Rotary Club Barbecue for Exhibitors

1:30 p.m.—Judging of Calves

3:00 p.m.—Judging of Hogs

4:00 p.m.—Judging of Sheep

7:00 p.m.—8:30 p.m.—All Livestock Exhibits Open to Public

7:00 p.m.—8:30 p.m.—Music by Allan Junior High School Band. J. M. Skrivanek, Director

8:30 p.m.—Award of Ribbons to All Winners

Friday, February 23

10:00 a.m.—Auction—To Be Broadcast over Local Stations. Public Auction of All Calves, Hogs, and Lambs Entered in the Junior Division of the Show. Special Auction of Registered Jersey Bull Calf Donated to the Junior Livestock Show by Joe C. Carrington.

1:30 p.m.—Kiwanis Club Barbecue for Exhibitors

1947
8TH ANNUAL
TRAVIS COUNTY
JUNIOR LIVESTOCK SHOW

•

FEATURING
4-H and FFA Fat Stock Show and
Auction Sale

•

AT
THE UNION STOCK YARDS
Austin, Texas

FEBRUARY 20 & 21, 1947

SPONSORED BY AUSTIN CHAMBER OF COMMERCE

The program cover from the 1947 show held at the Union Stock Yards. (AF-A1500(17), Austin History Center, Austin Public Library)

that the City of Austin purchased and had recently erected on city property called the Butler Tract. The Quonset hut, on Riverside Drive near downtown Austin, was surrounded largely by undeveloped land with the Missouri Pacific Railroad tracks and West Bouldin Creek to the west and Riverside Drive to the north. Disch Baseball Field sat to the south.

Capital Area Farm and Ranch Club Takes Over

When the annual exhibition moved into the Coliseum for what would become a long-term residency, the show finally had accommodations that allowed leaders to think big, or at least beyond Travis County. But to grow, it may have needed more funding than the chamber could provide, as well as a wider base of public support. For those or perhaps other reasons, the

R. E. Janes, A. G. Adams Jr., Fred S. Nagle Jr., and Joe C. Carrington. But until a new home could be found, the show moved to temporary headquarters at the Union Stock Yards, at 521 Pleasant Valley Road, for the 1947 and 1948 shows. John L. Moulden, manager of the yards, had assisted the chamber's Agricultural Bureau since the early 1940s and served in leadership roles with the show.

Finally, the show moved in 1949 into the City Coliseum, a former B-52 aircraft hanger

Austin City Coliseum. (ND-53–513, Austin History Center, Austin Public Library)

chamber helped form the Capital Area Farm and Ranch Club, which took over the show's sponsorship starting with the 1950 event. In its 1949 report, the chamber noted: "With this new organization, further impetus can be given to an agricultural show which will include not only Travis County but neighboring counties as well."

The club also took charge of many of the other agricultural development activities and outreach efforts made to surrounding communities that had been the responsibility of the chamber's Agricultural Bureau. The chamber assisted by providing administrative support to the club and the show. The Capital Area Farm and Ranch Club's membership came close to 200 during its first year. The show's new leadership and the larger venue of the Coliseum, which could seat just under 2,000, spurred the rapid expansion of the show (from 1949 to 1956) and the addition of entertainment—including a junior rodeo with evening musical entertainment and a small fair.

Starting as early as 1953, carnival rides, midway attractions, and farm and ranch exhibits set up around the Coliseum. That year, attendees could try their luck at ring toss or take a spin on a Ferris wheel set up just south of the Coliseum as part of the Don Franklin Midway from San Antonio. In 1954, a newspaper account mentioned Fort Worth carnival company Bill Hames Shows as a star attraction. The curious could line up to see the largest living twin Holstein steers and Mitzi, the smallest living cow (24 inches tall), or watch daredevil motorcyclists racing inside "the motordome."

Visitors in 1954 could also peruse antique and new cars, peer at penned Texas wildlife, and visit commercial exhibits. In 1955, these ranged from a mobile home show and military displays that included a U.S. Air Force plane, to a car show and exhibitors with goods for homemakers, farmers, and ranchers.

Tex Ritter Headlines Parade

The ambitious Capital Area Farm and Ranch Club in the early 1950s also kicked off the livestock show with a parade through the heart of downtown Austin. The Bergstrom Air Force Base Band led the mile-long procession of the first parade, held in 1952, followed by country-music singer and Western movie actor Tex Ritter atop his horse, White Flash.

Also during the early 1950s, the chamber's Retail Trade Development Committee promoted Go Western Week for the five days leading up to the show's kickoff. The campaign, which began in 1954 and apparently lasted only a few years (but was brought back in later decades), was meant to welcome visiting stock show participants and to promote the event to Austin residents. Everyone was encouraged to don jeans, boots, string ties, cowboy hats, and other Western garb. Downtown retailers competed for the best Western-themed window display.

The *Austin Statesman* reported in 1954 that city police sported bright blue string ties and everyone—from hotel bellboys, café waitresses, and office staff—wore their finest farm-and-ranch wear during Go Western Week. Photos by Neal Douglass (the originals long-since gone)

Exhibitors in the 1951 Travis County Junior Livestock Show pose with their winning animals and a show official near the City Coliseum. (ND-51–258, Austin History Center, Austin Public Library)

Young cowboys lounge on hay bales during the 1954 Travis County Junior Livestock Show while more hay is unloaded. (Russell Lee Collection, e_rl_0140_pub, The Dolph Briscoe Center for American History, The University of Texas at Austin)

accompanying the story show cowboy-hat-wearing Texas Highway Department secretaries in smart-looking pearl-snap Western shirts and knotted neckerchiefs.

Capital Area Livestock Show Broadens Scope

The change of the event's name to the *Capital Area Livestock Show* in 1952 reflected the exhibition's widened scope, which the chamber had envisioned four years earlier. The 1952 show grew for the first time to include three exhibitions in one: a Travis County junior live-stock show, an 11-county junior breeders show, and an open-class adult breeders show. The

Austin Statesman reported, "The exposition will be the biggest livestock show ever held here and the first area-wide agricultural event ever held in Austin." Stock arriving was expected to fill the sheds and three large tents erected adjacent to the Coliseum. Elgin High School student Curtis Neidig won grand champion that year with his 1,000-pound Hereford.

Dave Shanks not only covered the show as the farm-and-ranch editor at the Austin dailies, the *Austin American* and the *Austin Statesman*, but also crowed about the expanded event in his opinion column on ranch and farm issues titled "Reuben's Half Acre." "There is no single-shot way to incur area goodwill. But the 1952 Capital Area Livestock show is one way to boost the area and the city. And for that reason, the stock show is everybody's project. The support for the show this year has been generous," he wrote. He gave the bulk of the credit for the six-day event to L. N. Kirkpatrick, the event's general superintendent, "who is on loan from the Lower Colorado River Authority," and C. J. Schmid, president of the Capital Area Farm and Ranch Club.

In 1953, the show added two new competitions, the Capital Area Horse Show and the Capital Area Rabbit Show. A total premium purse of more than $5,000 was paid to show winners. According to the chamber's March 1953 *Austin in Action* newsletter, the show was open to junior breeders from all over Texas, "making Austin the first major show in the state to offer a complete state-wide Junior Breeders' Show."

The chamber announced that the 1954 show would be split. The first three days would be dedicated to adult breeders showing beef, dairy cattle, sheep, rabbits, and horses. The last three days would again include junior breeders from 4-H and FFA clubs statewide in addition to the Travis County youth showing fat steers, fat lambs, rabbits, sheep, and poultry.

Rapid Expansion Ends Abruptly

During these early years, the livestock show, fair, and rodeo reached a pinnacle in 1955. What had begun as a small, countywide calf show in 1940 had, in 15 years, grown into a seven-day production during which the livestock judged ranged from shorthorn and dairy cattle, quarter horses and palominos, to rabbits and sheep. In some livestock departments, entrants even came from out of state. The exhibition had expanded to include a mile-long parade, a junior rodeo, crowning of a rodeo queen, a slate of nationally known performers, a carnival midway, and a dozen or more educational and commercial exhibits.

But the Capital Area Farm and Ranch Club could not maintain the larger production it had worked so hard to develop. In 1956, the length of the livestock show was reduced to four days. The club dropped the rodeo entirely but staged a variety show in its place during the evenings. In Shanks's opinion, the size of the Coliseum was to blame: "The Coliseum, unyieldingly limited in its resources, finally has broken the back of the rodeo enthusiasts, who had worked hard to put on a small-size rodeo as part of the stock show. Even Bill Sandifer, the Manor squire and junior producer who 'toughed out' the horseless roping, pig scrambles, etc., hoping eventually for a break, isn't too sorry to see the junior rodeo pass."

It's easy to understand how the size of the Coliseum frustrated and limited rodeo producers. Although it's not entirely clear why the Capital Area Livestock Show suddenly retracted from its fast-paced expansion, one reason might be the searing drought that had the Great Plains and the southwestern United States in its grip during much of the 1950s. Texas

A judge examines horses during a 1954 competition in the City Coliseum. (Russell Lee Collection, di_07027, The Dolph Briscoe Center for American History, The University of Texas at Austin)

Spectators at the 1954 livestock show in the stands of the City Coliseum. (Russell Lee Collection, di_070206, The Dolph Briscoe Center for American History, The University of Texas at Austin)

A girl with her grand champion broilers at the 1956 show. (Russell Lee Collection, di_07030, The Dolph Briscoe Center for American History, The University of Texas at Austin)

A young exhibitor concentrates on hanging on to her sheep during the 1956 show. (Russell Lee Collection, e_rl_0166_pub, The Dolph Briscoe Center for American History, The University of Texas at Austin)

rainfall dropped by 40 percent between 1949 and 1951, and by 1953, 75 percent of Texas recorded below-normal rainfall. The record drought devastated the region's agriculture and only started to abate in 1957. By this time, 244 of the 254 counties in Texas had been declared federal drought disaster areas. Crop yields in some areas of the multistate region affected had dropped by as much as 50 percent, and high temperatures and low rainfall scorched grasslands typically used for grazing.

Surely the economic blows dealt by the drought adversely affected the philanthropy necessary to support the show, as well as the ability of individuals to raise and enter livestock and to attend from across the state. Perhaps the event just grew too quickly under the stewardship of the Capital Area Farm and Ranch Club. The multiple livestock classes and exhibits must have strained the Coliseum's limited facilities. For whatever reasons, the exhibition that had done so much in its first few years to advance the livestock industry in Travis County and the surrounding area had become financially unsustainable. 🥾

Otto Bohls, who served as superintendent of swine during the 1957 show. (Russell Lee Collection, di_07034, The Dolph Briscoe Center for American History, The University of Texas at Austin)

The Miss Rodeo Austin crown is worn on the queen's hat. (Courtesy Star of Texas Fair and Rodeo)

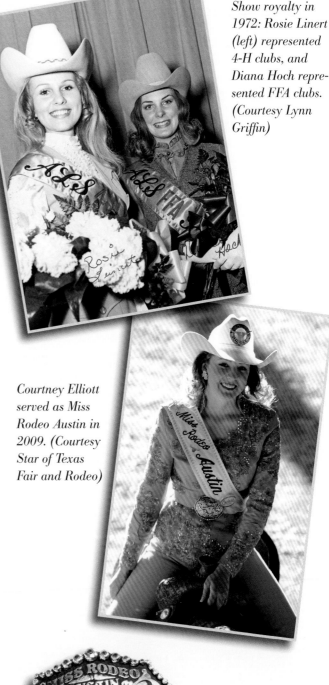

Austin Livestock Show royalty in 1972: Rosie Linert (left) represented 4-H clubs, and Diana Hoch represented FFA clubs. (Courtesy Lynn Griffin)

RODEO AND LIVESTOCK SHOW CROWN ROYALTY

The lineage of the Star of Texas Fair and Rodeo's rodeo royalty can be traced back to 1954, when the Travis County Junior Livestock Show crowned Janice Germany of Burnet as its first rodeo queen.

After the short-lived rodeo performances of the 1950s, the organization began to crown livestock royalty instead. At least by 1967, the honor bestowed was that of Austin Livestock Show Sweetheart. In 1969, the sweetheart contest appears to have become the Austin Livestock Show Princess contest in which 4-H and FFA girls from 24 counties competed for two crowns.

Scholarships were given to the winning girls for the first time in 1972, when they each received "a certificate denoting a $200 college scholarship to the college or university of their choice," according to the March 1974 issue of the chamber's magazine, Austin. The show also provided princesses with Western outfits—including suits, boots, and hats—and hosted them throughout the show. At least during the 1980s, the Austin–Travis County Livestock Show and Rodeo crowned both a rodeo queen and a livestock show princess.

Courtney Elliott served as Miss Rodeo Austin in 2009. (Courtesy Star of Texas Fair and Rodeo)

Today, the Star of Texas Fair and Rodeo holds an annual Miss Rodeo Austin Scholarship Contest in which Miss Rodeo Austin and Miss Rodeo Austin Princess are crowned. The winners are chosen based on their horsemanship, personality, and appearance and are awarded college scholarships of $16,000 and $10,000, respectively. The Star of Texas Fair and Rodeo also pays $300 toward Miss Rodeo Austin's registration fees for competition in the Miss Rodeo Texas Pageant.

In 2011, the Star of Texas Fair and Rodeo crowned Katie Crews of Texarkana as Miss Rodeo Austin and Stephanie Revels of Decatur as Miss Rodeo Austin Princess.

A jewel-encrusted Miss Rodeo Austin belt buckle. (Courtesy Star of Texas Fair and Rodeo)

In October 1956, the Capital Area Farm and Ranch Club was in debt, owing the City of Austin $1,592 for its lease of the Coliseum that year and, in an effort to save the livestock show, handed the event back into the hands of the Austin Chamber of Commerce. The chamber agreed to again sponsor the show, intending to run it on a self-financing basis. Lynn Griffin, the chamber's newly hired agricultural manager, handled the bulk of the work and coordinated with a board of directors to produce a two-day event in 1957. Rechristened the *Austin Livestock Show*, it was open only to Travis County youth. "They [the Capital Area Farm and Ranch Club] were losing money, so they decided to let it go," recalled Griffin. "I put together a premium list for a county show, just for 4-H and FFA kids."

Griffin relied upon youth involved with the event to serve as show boosters. Reviving a program that had been instituted in 1944, the chamber established a board of junior directors to help lead the event and its promotion. In 1957, youth board members spent two weeks speaking before Austin civic and service clubs and urging city merchants and residents to visit the show and bid during the livestock auction.

The scaled-down exhibition continued to include cattle, lamb, pig, poultry, and rabbit entries. Entertainment scheduled was also much more conservative than in years past, with the Jackson Brewing Company's radio bands performing daytime concerts on the show grounds.

Steady Growth under Chamber Sponsorship

Downsizing the show to its roots as a county-wide youth competition and once again relying upon the chamber's sponsorship ensured that

An Austin Livestock Show judge talks to a group of boys as he inspects a bird during the 1957 show. A junior director for the show appears in the upper right. (Russell Lee Collection, di_07025, The Dolph Briscoe Center for American History, The University of Texas at Austin)

Boys and girls lead their steers around the ring during judging at the 1957 show. (Russell Lee Collection, di_07033, The Dolph Briscoe Center for American History, The University of Texas at Austin)

Austin Chamber of Commerce Agricultural Manager Lynn Griffin (second from right), a representative from the Butter Crust Bakery (second from left), and an unidentified man pose with a boy and his winning steer during the early 1960s. (Courtesy Lynn Griffin)

the event continued. During the 1957 show, the chamber was able to pay premiums to the winners, cover its costs, and emerge with a small surplus. The Austin Livestock Show not only survived that year but during the following two decades slowly grew to once again become a multicounty livestock show, with a rodeo, musical entertainment, and a fair.

The number of livestock exhibits had initially decreased when the chamber took over the show, but the group immediately rebuilt the event to 265 entries in 1957 and 383 in 1958. Show departments in 1959 grew to include fat steers; fat lambs; fat barrows (castrated male pigs); poultry; rabbits; beef cattle; registered dairy cattle; purebred, nonregistered dairy cattle; registered ewes; purebred, nonregistered ewes; registered rams; purebred Angora doe goats; and registered gilts (young female pigs). A commercial steer show joined the schedule in 1960, as did a commercial lamb show in 1961. In 1963, the chamber erected two 30-by-60-foot tents to help house the growing number of entries, reported Clark Bolt in the *Austin American-Statesman*'s Farm Roundup column. "The fact is, a third tent is needed to handle the overflow, but costs prevent this," Bolt noted.

The Austin Farm and Ranch Club formed in 1964. Although similar in name to the Capital Area Farm and Ranch Club that had run the show from 1949 to 1956, this group did not take over entire sponsorship of the event. Its members appear to have worked with the chamber to help provide financial and volunteer support to the show and to other agriculture-boosting projects.

A judge inspects sheep during the 1957 show as spectators watch inside the City Coliseum. (Russell Lee Collection, di_07032, The Dolph Briscoe Center for American History, The University of Texas at Austin)

Perhaps it was with the club's assistance that the show was able in 1965 to grow again into a multicounty event: a competition for Travis County junior exhibitors and an adult open competition for breeders from Travis, Williamson, Burnet, Llano, Blanco, Hays, Caldwell, Bastrop, and Lee counties. The event was free, and organizers expected 25,000 attendees. Stockmen visiting the exhibition that year commented that many of the entries (1,126 in all) had been shown on the larger stock show circuit (in Fort Worth, San Antonio, and Houston). A new barn constructed by the City of Austin at the west end of the Coliseum helped accommodate the additional animals. Show organizers also relied upon tents, some of them heated, to house informational exhibits and animals.

The 1965 event had a record premium purse

of $5,000 for Travis County junior exhibit winners and $10,000 for the open breeders division winners. During the auction, the grand champion 834-pound Hereford, shown by Gordon "Buddy" Smith of Del Valle, brought $2.05 per pound from Harry Akin of the Night Hawk Restaurants. (Akin had purchased the grand champion calf 25 years earlier in 1940.) The restaurant owner promptly resold the steer to Big Bear Food Store for $500.40 ($0.60 per pound) and gave the cash to the Austin Community Guidance Center.

In 1966, the burgeoning show offered a total of $16,000 in prize money and expanded

Gordon Smith and his grand champion steer in 1967 with a representative from Safeway Stores. Smith's animal was purchased for $3,397.60 by the Barn Restaurant, which resold it to Safeway Stores for $0.41 per pound. The resale proceeds were donated to the following year's show. (PICA 00021, Austin History Center, Austin Public Library)

to six days, with organizers adding a Red Angus beef department to the open division and an Angora buck goat department to the junior show. Horses again were part of the program—including 4-H and FFA horse shows, a national cutting horse competition, and an open quarter horse competition.

The nine-day exhibition expanded again in 1967, this time to 1,500 entries. In addition to the traditional Travis County junior show for steers, lambs, hogs, poultry, and rabbits, it added new adult and junior breeder competitions now open to a 23-county area. The counties included were Travis, Williamson, Lee, Bastrop, Caldwell, Hays, Blanco, Llano, Burnet, Lampasas, Bell, Milam, Burleson, Washington, Fayette, Gonzales, Guadalupe, Comal, Kendall, Gillespie, Mason, McCullough, and San Saba. Breeding animals entered included beef cattle, dairy cattle, sheep, goats, and swine.

Griffin, quoted in the chamber's *Austin* magazine in March 1967, said further expansion of the show was not likely "until we get a new coliseum or necessary facilities." Asked today, he recalled, "It was a Mickey Mouse place to have a stock show; that's all I can say. Starting around 1964–65 we just rented an extra tent. We had one tent to put all the sheep and goats and rabbits, and a tent for the children's barnyard. We kept the cattle and pigs inside."

Despite the limits of the Coliseum, event organizers during the late 1960s and 1970s managed to incorporate additional horse shows and accommodate more livestock. Appaloosa and cutting horse shows began in 1968; a youth quarter horse competition was added in 1971;

CHAPTER **3**

and a paint horse show, in 1973. In 1978, youth livestock exhibits alone climbed to 1,500, and adult exhibits reached 1,000. The rabbit and poultry exhibitions had to be housed in the Municipal Auditorium's basement, just southeast of the Coliseum, that year. The chamber also reestablished the rodeo-type competitions as well as the evening concerts and exhibits that attendees had first enjoyed during the event's heyday in the 1950s.

Rodeo Entertainment Added

The last junior rodeo was held in 1955 when the Capital Area Farm and Ranch Club was in charge of the show. When the chamber took over show sponsorship in 1957, the organization not only scaled back the livestock exhibits but also further cut the associated entertainment and fair. But by 1958 it once again hosted a few rodeo-type events—a pig scramble, as well as goat scramble and goat sacking and tying competitions. Selection of the grand champion steer and a "parade of champions" also became part of the evening productions. But as the show continued to expand the entertainment offered during the 1960s, the Coliseum's limited facilities again became a problem. When Buck Owens performed as part of livestock show events in 1965, his concert was staged in the larger, nearby Municipal Auditorium.

An *Austin American* special section about the 1963 livestock show states that the chamber hoped to one day have a larger facility in which it could host a "money-making rodeo" to cover the costs of the show. Working within their space restrictions, organizers expanded the evening shows. In 1967, calf roping and dogging competitions and a father-and-son calf roping contest drew spectators. Adults and children paid $0.50 and $0.10, respectively, to enter the show grounds.

Organizers again launched a rodeo in 1969. Amateur cowboys and cowgirls were invited to compete in the City Coliseum's small arena. Cecil Hill of Oak Hill produced the three-night event, which cost $1.75 for general admission. The rodeo became an annual event, and the Austin Livestock Show was then often referred to as the *Austin Livestock Show and Rodeo* (ALS&R).

By at least the early 1960s, Bill Hames Shows and Bob Hammond Shows provided carnival midways and rides on the fairgrounds just south of the Coliseum. Griffin said the carnival provided needed income: "We did pretty well [financially] on the carnival," he said, remembering that he accepted only cash for carnival receipts. "I'd hide the cash over at the chamber office. One year I had $26,000, and I called the bank to let them know I was bringing in the deposit. The teller said, 'You just stay there. We'll come and get it.'" Griffin said that he established a children's barnyard in the early 1960s as part of the annual event, a special attraction for the droves of children touring the grounds.

By 1975, the carnival rides, games of chance, and concessions were open 10 days. About 1978, the Thomas Carnival set up its midway, said Ted Nagel, who first joined the show's board in 1974, then served as show president in 1981. "Probably one of our best transitions was get-

Financial Support Fuels Dream of Larger Home

Even though the exhibition and attractions were growing—a parade down Congress Avenue was added in 1979 to kick off the 10-day festivities—the Coliseum's lack of space curbed the event's ability to expand further. Show organizers had during the 1960s and 1970s creatively made do with the facility while consistently lobbying—alongside dozens of civic organizations and individuals—that Austin needed a new coliseum and convention center.

Generous gifts made by retired Austin businessman and philanthropist Louis J. Luedecke, a longtime supporter of area youth and the livestock show, kept alive the hope for a larger facility during the 1970s. As early as 1951, farm-and-ranch editor Dave Shanks of the Austin *American* and *Statesman* newspapers wrote,

> Luedecke can be credited for the strong show made by the Shorthorn breed at the 1951 show. . . . Luedecke comes into the act by helping interested club boys and girls find suitable calves and by adding a rather whopping amount to the special prizes in the Shorthorn division. Luedecke offered $100, $75, and $50 for the first three ranking Shorthorns. He added $75 if the best Shorthorn won the grand championship and was shown by a girl and $50 if the Shorthorn won the grand championship and was won by a boy. He offered $50 across the board if the reserve champion steer was a Shorthorn.

The Austin Livestock Show and Rodeo dedicated its 1971 show to philanthropist Louis J. Luedecke (far left). Standing with him (left to right) are Jim Boswell of Austin National Bank and Austin Chamber Agricultural Manager Lynn Griffin. An unidentified woman also helps at the ribbon cutting to open the show. (Courtesy Lynn Griffin)

Both Griffin and Verlin Callahan, show president in 1972 and 1973, recall Luedecke donating to the Lanier High School FFA club in the 1960s and worked closely with him to encourage his support for the Austin show. In the early 1970s Luedecke gave the chamber property that was to be sold for livestock show capital improvements. In 1971, the chamber dedicated the show to Luedecke.

The *Austin Statesman* account of the dedication ceremony stated that the 89-year-old "for a quarter of a century has given his support to rural youth in the area." When the philanthropist died in 1976, the chamber put Luedecke's donations into a trust, and that seed money allowed the show's organizers to start thinking seriously about constructing a new, much larger facility. Meanwhile, during the 1970s the ever-expanding enterprise often either generated only a small profit or large deficits after paying its bills. "We were losing money, and we didn't know if we were going to survive," said Nagel.

The Travis County Commissioners had been providing financial support to the show as early as 1966. Show organizers beseeched the Commissioners Court in the late 1970s to step up assistance. The plea worked. "Travis County came in and gave us $25,000," Nagel said. "When Travis County started substantially funding the show, I told the chamber we need to change the name," Verlin Callahan said. "We got to the point where the county was going to tell us to go stick it." Starting with the 1979 event, the Austin Livestock Show and Rodeo became the *Austin–Travis County Livestock Show and Rodeo* (ATCLS&R) and was on the verge of breaking away from the chamber. 🥾

Program cover of the 1976 event. (Courtesy Star of Texas Fair and Rodeo)

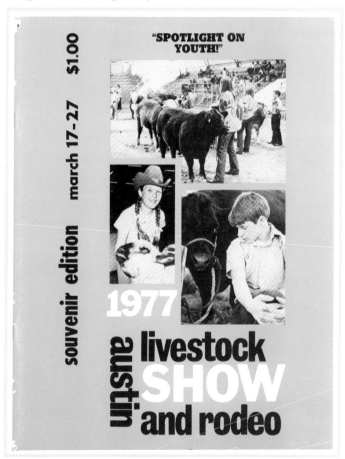

Program cover of the 1977 event. (Courtesy Star of Texas Fair and Rodeo)

SUPPORTERS KEY TO SUCCESS

What do the Driskill Hotel, the Night Hawk Restaurants, Dodge Ram trucks, and Sprint all have in common? How about a Round Rock bank manager, a Central Texas pecan farmer, a Southwest Airlines pilot, and a registered nurse? These supporters and others, giving thousands of hours of hard work and millions of dollars in cash and in-kind donations, have helped for more than 70 years turn the small Baby Beef Show for Travis County youth into one of Central Texas' largest nonprofit charities, the Star of Texas Fair and Rodeo.

Volunteers

Even in its early days, the small livestock show sponsored by the Austin Chamber of Commerce relied greatly upon help from volunteers. In 1945, more than a hundred members of 11 volunteer committees helped the chamber's Agricultural Bureau stage the show, handling everything from the awards and publicity to managing the grounds, records, and sales.

Austin civic clubs also chipped in where they could. The Austin Rotary Club served barbecue to more than 200 people during the first day of the 1945 exhibition, and the Austin Kiwanis Club hosted the hungry crowd on day two. In 1948, the Lions Club not only provided donations that paid for photographs of the champion animals with their owners but also gave cash prizes. This early involvement by Austin civic clubs heralded years of support these groups provided, including trips members

made to area towns such as Manor, Elgin, and Giddings in the 1950s to promote the event.

Members of the Capital Area Farm and Ranch Club took over sponsorship of the show from 1950 to 1956. Very little information about this club is available, but enterprising members added a parade and rodeo and also expanded the livestock show during its stewardship.

At times, volunteers have been asked to sacrifice above and beyond what was normally expected for the organization to reach especially hard-to-attain goals. During the winter and spring of 1983–84, many laid flooring, wielded screwdrivers, or drove tractors alongside construction workers at night and on weekends to help raise the Texas Exposition and Heritage Center. Jimmy Callahan, president in 1983, served as the volunteer board member in charge of constructing the new facility, which allowed the Austin–Travis County Livestock Show and Rodeo to move out of the City Coliseum's cramped quarters in central Austin to the more spacious Expo Center grounds in northeast Austin just in time to produce its 1984 events.

Today, the charity has its own full-time, 14-member staff that is supplemented by hundreds of seasonal workers and contractors. But an army of more than 1,500 volunteers serving on 29 committees takes charge to produce dozens of the Star of Texas Fair and Rodeo's competitive and fund-raising events and other activities. From the calf scramble, the gala, and the golf tournament to ticket sales, animal care,

The Top Hand Award goes to the Star of Texas Fair and Rodeo's Volunteer of the Year. (Courtesy Star of Texas Fair and Rodeo)

"I like working with people, solving their problems, and making everything come together," said Berdoll, the organization's 2008 Volunteer of the Year. "It's rewarding when you see the place the way it is, and then, two weeks after we take over the property, you've got a city set up and running smoothly." Interacting with children and their parents participating in the livestock show is especially rewarding, he said. "You'll see kids that are showing an animal for the first time. They'll be so proud and start talking to you about their animal and how much fun they are having," Berdoll said. "You walk through that barn almost every day, and you're going to have a parent say 'we just enjoy y'all's show so much.' It makes you feel good when they come out and thank you for the show and for helping them out."

Participants in the livestock show during their school days in the 1990s, Shelley Talley and her sister, Becky Silco, now pitch in, alongside other family members, to assist in the show barn annually. "I love to volunteer," Talley said. "If I can give back just a little of what these people gave me, it's a blessing to say the least." "The barn really is a family project," Silco said. "And for our family a project that is twenty-five years and counting."

Fred Weber, president in 2012, said he is frequently amazed by the hard work and level of commitment from the charity's volunteers. "They give all of this time. It's incredible," Weber said. "They are all about being a part of this show and helping kids. To me that is the most fantastic thing. So many of them will work so hard to be on a committee, and it's amazing the ownership that they take."

and legal and safety issues, volunteers are generous with their leadership, expertise, and time. Many take two weeks of vacation from their jobs every March to work the fairgrounds, erecting pens in the livestock barn, checking in hogs and their owners at 3:00 a.m., or trouble-shooting the myriad issues that can surface during such a large event.

Each March, pecan farmer Keith Berdoll leads a small crew of Operations Committee volunteers who practically live on the grounds for almost a month. The group readies the usually deserted site and its buildings to host the coming onslaught of participants and spectators. Once events kick off, the group solves problems—fixing parking snarls, repairing burst water pipes, and wrangling fugitive llamas back to the petting zoo—into the wee hours.

Volunteers flip pancakes at the 2008 cowboy breakfast at Auditorium Shores. The annual event kicks off the organization's myriad activities each March. (Courtesy Star of Texas Fair and Rodeo)

The organization's presidents and its more than 80 board members are all volunteers as well. The board includes past presidents who remain involved, some for up to three decades, as well as new board members with only a half-dozen years under their belts.

Shaun Tuggle, show president in 2008, started as a volunteer on the Commercial Exhibits Committee when he got out of college in 1987. Today he sits on several committees. Tuggle recalled that he first got involved with the organization as a way to meet new people and develop business connections. But after

serving on the Calf Scramble Committee, he realized the importance of the organization's work and his contributions to it when watching the work performed by youth after they won certificates to purchase calves to raise and show. "The kids showing projects have to feed and care for their animals early every morning and every evening, even on holidays," Tuggle said. "They learn dedication, commitment, responsibility, and financial recordkeeping. They're learning valuable life skills. That's when I swallowed the hook. That's when I really got engaged and went 'wow,'" Tuggle said. "This whole thing that we do—the rodeo, stock show, carnival, dances, and everything— it's all to help to these kids."

"The 1,500 volunteers are the heart and soul of the organization," said Bucky Lamb, chief executive officer of the organization. "Yet behind every volunteer stand family members and friends who offer support and encouragement."

Bidders and Buyers Groups

Those who bid on and purchase students' projects—whether they are fattened calves and pigs, hand-tooled leather belts, or oil paintings—have always been crucial supporters. During the original Baby Beef Show, those purchasing FFA and 4-H students' calves helped youth pocket rewards for their efforts while supporting the chamber's mission to educate area residents about the proper care and feeding of these animals. In those early years, the Driskill Hotel, the Night Hawk Restaurants, Kash-Karry Stores, and other iconic Austin businesses often purchased animals. In 1949 alone, more than 60 Austin companies spent over $17,000 on animals at the auction.

Over time, additional livestock competitions were added, and the number of bidders grew. By 1973, steer, pig, sheep, and poultry buyers—including Louis J. Luedecke, Night Hawk Restaurants, City National Bank, and Austin Beer Distributors—paid over $113,500 for 240 animals.

An exhibitor leads his steer around the ring as the auctioneer takes bids during the 1956 show in the City Coliseum. (Russell Lee Collection, di_07029, The Dolph Briscoe Center for American History, The University of Texas at Austin)

Students who competed in the youth fair during the early 1980s through 2005 could pocket sales receipts during the auction of their creations—from pickled beets and layer cakes to stained glass and metal outdoor furniture. And since 2006, bidders have vied to purchase winning artwork produced by students competing in the organization's Western art competition. In 2011, youth Western art projects generated $15,550 for 20 aspiring artists.

Starting with the 500 Club in 1980, buyers groups were formed to help drive up bids and ensure the best prices are paid to all youth at the auction. Club members donated $500 annually. "The county agents and ag teachers would tell us which kids worked hard and were from families that didn't have much," recalled Mike Levi, who joined the 500 Club upon becoming a board member in the early 1980s. "That's where we would concentrate our purchases during the sale. That gave us a great deal of

Bidders, photographers, and spectators focus on a boy and his steer during the 1978 livestock auction. (Courtesy Star of Texas Fair and Rodeo)

pleasure, because we were helping kids who needed it most." Levi served as president in 1990.

The 500 Club became the Presidents' Club and continues to this day. "It's the support group that helps establish the floor for the sale," said Jay Evans, club member and president in 1979 and 1985. "Most of the time the Presidents' Club starts the bidding, and if it gets up to an acceptable level, they'll let somebody else make the purchase. We still focus on purchasing projects from kids we feel have a special need. The Presidents' Club has raised well over $650,000 since it began."

Some of the larger buyers groups active today include Oink Inc., Pappa Cluck and the Cluckers, BBQ Buyers Group, Bell County Buyers Group, the Goathounds, the Lone Star Cattlemen, and the High Tech Buyers Group.

Individual buyers continue to make a huge impact as well. Longtime philanthropist and supporter of Texas youth Richard Wallrath set a new record in 2001 when he bid $102,000 for the grand champion steer raised by Brittany Barton of Jarrell High School. The following year Mike McCarty of McCarty Corporation set the existing record when he bid $107,000 for the grand champion steer exhibited by Mary Perry of Gillespie County 4-H. The record still stood as of 2011. Buyers at the 2011 auction included H-E-B, KST Electric, and McCarty. Doug Maund purchased the grand champion steer from Cuatro Schauer for $60,000.

Dear 500 Club,

I appreciate your organizations purchasing my livestock animals. The money will help me to participate in next year's livestock show. Thanks again and see ya next year!

Sincerely,

A grateful student in the 1980s penned this letter to the 500 Club. (Courtesy Star of Texas Fair and Rodeo)

The top 10 highest bidders at the annual youth livestock auction receive awards such as this one. (Courtesy Star of Texas Fair and Rodeo)

In-Kind Donors, Sponsors, and Other Supporters

In-kind donations as well as funds from donors and sponsors have been very important. The Austin Chamber of Commerce tops the list in providing the first in-kind support. It sponsored the original livestock show and provided at least one staff member to help organize and run the show for more than three decades.

In addition, from 1942 to 1946, the City of Austin let the chamber hold its show at the Municipal Market House, apparently for no charge. The city even furnished free processing of auctioned animals at the Municipal Abattoir. In 1947 and 1948, the Union Stock Yards hosted the growing show, also for free.

Other in-kind support over the years includes workers and equipment provided by the Travis County Commissioners Court and materials and labor donated and provided at cost by numerous companies during the building of the Travis County Expo Center. Firms cited by the chamber in the March 1984 issue of *Austin* magazine include Faulkner Construction, J. C. Evans Construction, Capitol Equipment, and Texas Ready Mix.

Sponsorships have helped provide publicity for the livestock show and its associated events and even ensured that particular events occur. In 1944, more than 60 Austin businesses and individuals—including Mayor Tom Miller and University of Texas President Homer P. Rainey—sponsored a full-page ad in the *Austin Statesman* touting the livestock show and auction.

During the calf scramble competition in 1949, calf donors included Arthur Ashford of Western Reserve Life Insurance Company, dairyman Herman Heep, and Fred Catterall of Walker Austex Chili Company. The Austin American-Statesman continued to sponsor the scramble for several years. In 1950, the agile scramblers went home with Aberdeen Angus calves worth $1,500. The scramble started up again in 1984, and the Austin–Travis County Livestock Show and Rodeo's 1985 program lists 50 sponsors, including Texas Instruments, Allens Boot Center, and First National Bank of Bastrop, each of whom donated $500 to supply certificates to scramble winners for the purchase of calves to raise for competition at next year's show.

Today, recruiting sponsors is an even bigger part of the Star of Texas Fair and Rodeo's development efforts. "As the organization's scope has evolved, local sponsors have been complemented with a growing number of national corporate sponsors," said Katy Blankinship, senior manager. "Corporate sponsors have played a significant role in the explosive growth of our scholarship program and total charitable giving."

Annually, sponsorships account for more than 18 percent of the charity's total annual income. Support comes from more than 50 businesses, including Dodge Ram trucks, H-E-B, State Farm, Dell, and Austin Foam Plastics. Several individuals, businesses, and organizations have provided significant contributions over the years that have helped out the organization at times of particular need. Among these is Travis County, whose commissioners at least as early as 1966 voted to appropriate funds to assist the show.

The Lower Colorado River Authority gave the Austin–Travis County Livestock Show and Rodeo a $100,000 grant in 1998 to construct a logistical command center to be used during its annual events. In 2006, longtime show supporter Charles W. Graham, a nationally renowned Central Texas veterinarian, donated $100,000 in seed money to the charity to construct its current office near the Expo Center grounds, which is named Dr. Charles W. Graham Western Heritage Center in his honor.

There is no way to tally the total amount given by individuals and institutions to the organization over its long history. Today, whether someone writes a check for a multi-thousand-dollar donation, bids on silent auction items at the annual gala, or buys rodeo tickets, all contributions to the organization make a difference. "Everything we receive in the way of individuals' time or through generous donations helps us further our efforts to promote youth education and preserve Western heritage," Bucky Lamb said. "Everything counts."

Philanthropist Louis J. Luedecke. (Courtesy Star of Texas Fair and Rodeo)

Ardent show supporter Louis J. Luedecke in 1970 gave 21.5 acres of land, on what was then called the Bastrop Highway in southeast Austin, to the chamber with instructions that proceeds from its sale be given to the livestock show for capital improvements. In 1971, Luedecke also gave the chamber a house and lot on Manor Road to be sold and the money used for the same purpose. The trust established from the sales of these properties helped create the $350,000 in seed money that enabled the show to build the Travis County Expo Center. The arena bears his name today.

Luedecke (1881–1976), born in Manor, was the eldest son of Travis County pioneers Emma H. and William Luedecke. According to his obituary in the *Austin American-Statesman*, the philanthropist was a graduate of Texas Lutheran College. He worked as manager of the Mutual Lumber Company of Bartlett before working with the International Harvester Company in Texas and Mexico. In 1932, he retired to attend to his and his family's interests following the death of his father. In addition to supporting the show and its participants, he gave generously to area 4-H and FFA clubs and to the Central Texas Boys Ranch. Livestock show directors dedicated their annual events to Luedecke in both 1971 and 1984.

The 1980s were exciting and tumultuous times for the Austin–Travis County Livestock Show and Rodeo (ATCLS&R). The organization revised and strengthened its bylaws, strengthened the rules governing its livestock show, and expanded its connections within the community. Also during this decade, show volunteers and donors were asked to step up and support the organization more than they ever had before.

A New Level of Maturity

Many longtime show directors credit Austin attorney Robert Sneed, an ardent show supporter and its president in 1980, as playing an important role in helping the organization mature during this time. "Mr. Sneed was for many years one of the most respected insurance and lobbying attorneys in the city of Austin," said Bill Knolle, who served as show president in 1984. "He knew everyone at the Capitol, and everybody knew him."

Sneed was born in McKinney in 1923, served with honors in World War II, and graduated from the Law School at the University of Texas at Austin in 1946. According to his obituary in the January 15, 2008, *Austin American-Statesman*, he was a partner in the Sneed, Vine, and Perry law firm, serving as an expert in zoning, land title, and insurance law. He also raised Simmental cattle in Blanco County. Sneed served as Travis County Democratic Party chairman from 1966 to 1972 and was known for his keen political sense. The Texas legislature recognized him on his seventieth birthday for his many contributions to state government.

Jay Evans, show president in both 1979 and

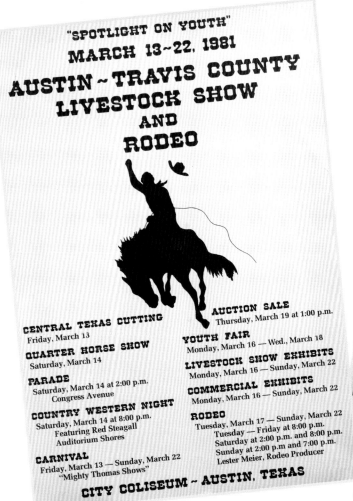

"SPOTLIGHT ON YOUTH"
MARCH 13~22, 1981
AUSTIN~TRAVIS COUNTY
LIVESTOCK SHOW
AND
RODEO

CENTRAL TEXAS CUTTING
Friday, March 13

QUARTER HORSE SHOW
Saturday, March 14

PARADE
Saturday, March 14 at 2:00 p.m.
Congress Avenue

COUNTRY WESTERN NIGHT
Saturday, March 14 at 8:00 p.m.
Featuring Red Steagall
Auditorium Shores

CARNIVAL
Friday, March 13 — Sunday, March 22
"Mighty Thomas Shows"

AUCTION SALE
Thursday, March 19 at 1:00 p.m.

YOUTH FAIR
Monday, March 16 — Wed., March 18

LIVESTOCK SHOW EXHIBITS
Monday, March 16 — Sunday, March 22

COMMERCIAL EXHIBITS
Monday, March 16 — Sunday, March 22

RODEO
Tuesday, March 17 — Sunday, March 22
Tuesday — Friday at 8:00 p.m.
Saturday at 2:00 p.m. and 8:00 p.m.
Sunday at 2:00 p.m and 7:00 p.m.
Lester Meier, Rodeo Producer

CITY COLISEUM ~ AUSTIN, TEXAS

This 1981 poster details the growing list of events held in conjunction with the livestock show. (Courtesy Star of Texas Fair and Rodeo)

AUSTIN~TRAVIS COUNTY
LIVESTOCK SHOW &
RODEO
MARCH 19-28
CITY COLISEUM

CENTRAL TEXAS CUTTING
Friday, March 19 at 6:00 P.M.

CARNIVAL
"Mighty Thomas Shows"
Friday, March 19~28
All Afternoon & Evening

COUNTRY WESTERN DANCES
Friday, March 19, 8:00~12:00 P.M.
Moe Bandy & the Rodeo Clowns &
The Metheny Brothers
Saturday, March 20, 8:00~12:00 P.M.
Gene Watson & the Farewell Party

BARBECUE
"The First Texas Invitational BBQ Cook Off"
Saturday, March 20
12:00~4:00 P.M.—Frenchie Burke

QUARTER HORSE SHOW
Saturday, March 20, 8:00 A.M., All day

COMMERCIAL EXHIBITS Friday, March 19~28

PARADE
Saturday, March 20, 2:00 P.M.
Congress Ave.

CROSS COUNTRY HORSE RACE
Sunday, March 21, 12:00 Noon

RODEO
Sunday, March 21~28
Lester Meier, Rodeo Producer

YOUTH FAIR
Tuesday, March 23~24
Auction, Wednesday, March 24, 4:00 P.M.

LIVESTOCK AUCTION
Thursday, March 25, 12:30 P.M.

LIVESTOCK EXHIBITS
Monday, March 22~Sunday, March 28

GET YOUR "KICKER" DISCOUNT PIN AT MANY LOCAL STORES.....
For information: call Chamber of Commerce 478-9383

This 1982 poster includes a barbecue cook-off and cross-country horse race, which were added to the schedule. (Courtesy Star of Texas Fair and Rodeo)

1985, credited Sneed with recruiting representatives from the Austin American-Statesman, the Travis County Commissioners Court, and other organizations from across the community to serve on the show board. "I think that brought a maturity and an approach that we didn't have before," Evans said. Evans also noted that Sneed helped create sound bylaws for the show's board of directors, spurred the group to

reach out regularly to the minority community, and emphasized that the group's mission was to support young people.

"The year I was president, Robert Sneed suggested we start doing scholarships," said Ted Nagel, who served as show president in 1981. "I appointed a committee to handle it." Providing college scholarships to outstanding students would grow to become the heart of the organization's mission.

Building a New Home: 1980 to 1989

In 1980, Sneed also created the first buyers group—the 500 Club (now known as the Presidents' Club)—to raise funds to spur bidding and buy animals during the livestock auction, ensuring that the youth would get a good price for their entries.

In the early 1980s the Austin Chamber of Commerce continued to sponsor the show and provided an executive director and a part-time administrative assistant. Kenneth Hees served as executive director from 1980 through the 1985 show. Hees said he took over from chamber employee Art Keller, who worked on the livestock show part-time during the 1970s after Lynn Griffin left the chamber in 1974.

The ATCLS&R's premium book, which contains the rules for raising and showing livestock, also reached a new level of maturity in the early 1980s. Show leaders strengthened the rules in response to events during the 1980 show. Board members suspected that adults had been too involved in caring for some children's winning animals, so the board withheld prize money from those contestants. The controversy lasted several months, prompting an investigation by the show board and the Del Valle Board of Education. In addition, the show board rewrote the rules governing substances that were prohibited from being administered to show animals.

Volunteers continued to be essential to the organization, and in 1980, ATCLS&R had 19 separate volunteer committees responsible for everything from staging the livestock auction, the junior horse and quarter horse shows, and the rodeo to organizing the parade, managing building and grounds issues, and handling public relations.

Branching Out

The livestock show and rodeo in the early 1980s was maxing out the limited space of the City Coliseum and its adjacent grounds. With a seating capacity of just under 2,000, the arena restricted the size and type of rodeo that could be held, as well as the musical acts that could be booked, which limited income from ticket sales. But show leaders and other volunteers made the most of the situation. Hees said the show added open junior beef heifer and dairy shows as well as an area commercial steer show in 1982. Other new activities introduced at this time broadened youth participation and public attendance, increased awareness of the organization and its mission, and helped build scholarship funds. Intentionally or not, these features also laid the necessary foundation upon which to build community support for solving a long-term problem—the show's need for a new, larger home.

A youth fair, begun in 1980, reached out to kids who might not have the ability to purchase and raise a show animal and, as a result, aided a cross section of residents the ATCLS&R had not previously touched. Students entered their projects in categories ranging from baked foods and pickles to metal crafts, tables, and barbecue grills. Jimmy Callahan, who headed up the event's first volunteer committee, recalled that projects were displayed in Palmer Auditorium southeast of the City Coliseum. (Palmer has since been renovated and is now the Long Center for the Performing Arts.) "[It] brought in a lot of kids that could participate in the show but who couldn't raise a sheep, couldn't raise a hog, couldn't do turkeys or chickens," said Callahan, who also served as show president in 1983. "So it brought in a whole new group of people. It was a big turning point."

The youth fair gave dozens of competitors, some of whom were at risk for dropping out of school or who had learning disabilities, the opportunity to learn the same lessons about responsibility, record keeping, and free enterprise as their fellow students raising and showing livestock. Kids competed for prizes and the chance to sell their projects at auction. "I think I came up with the youth fair auction idea [the second year the youth fair was held], and it just mushroomed after that," Jimmy Callahan said. Records from the early 1980s illustrate that dozens of kids from towns such as Creedmoor and Manchaca went home with $50 to $550 from the sales of their work.

It appears the show held non-livestock exhibitions for youth as early as 1958, when the chamber reported in *Austin in Action* that "a new feature of the show was the twenty educational booths which were set up by 4-H and FHA girls." The show schedule of events for

March 14, 1961, includes "Judging of Girls' Educational Exhibits." In 1978, the show included a two-day "homemakers' educational showcase" spread out in the basement of the Municipal Auditorium. Members of 4-H, FFA, and FHA submitted projects, including arts and crafts, needlework, potted plants, and canned and baked foods.

Starting in 1982, Verlin Callahan began to host ATCLS&R's first cross-country horse races on his ranch near Austin. These thrilling events continued through 1984. The action-packed competition included rescue races that pitted Travis County Sheriff's Office deputies against members of the Austin Police Department, 440-

A: '1 8, 1983

Dear Mr. Robert C. Sneed,

I would like to Thank you very much for buying my latch-hook rug at the 1983 2nd Annual Youth Fair Auction. I really do appreciate this kind thought.

This is my last year in the Youth Fair since I am a senior and will be graduating from Pflugerville High School next month. I would like to Thank you once again and I hope you will continue to show your willingness and fine support to us (today's Youth) in the years to come.

Thank you very much,

Tammy L. Heine

Tammy L. Heine

In 1980, the organization started a youth fair to feature non-livestock entries. Tammy Heine wrote to thank Robert Sneed for his purchase of her 1983 project. (Courtesy Star of Texas Fair and Rodeo)

yard races for men and women, an open derby horse race (with a $750 purse in 1983), and a race featuring local media celebrities.

Another first for 1982 was the show's inaugural barbecue cook-off. Bob Byland with Centex Beverage spearheaded this fund-raiser, which continues today. The *Austin American-Statesman* reported that contestants set up their smoking barbecue rigs on the former site of the Armadillo World Headquarters, at the southeast corner of Barton Springs Road and South First Street. Thirty teams invited from across Texas competed for a $1,000 jackpot while the hungry crowd nibbled barbecued brisket to the strains of Cajun music played by fiddler Frenchie Burke. Louisianan Burke entertained cook-off contestants in 1982 and for a number of subsequent years.

Judges at the first cook-off included author and comedian John Henry Faulk, radio personality Cactus Pryor, actor Guich Koock, *Austin American-Statesman* columnists Townsend Miller and Nat Henderson, and two representatives from the Houston Livestock Show's barbecue cook-off.

When local radio stations KVET and KOKE partnered with organizers in the early 1980s to stage country-and-western dances on Auditorium Shores on Austin's Town Lake, the show was able to provide musical entertainment to larger groups than it could host inside the confines of the Coliseum. Performer Gene Watson drew crowds in 1982 and 1983 with his chart-topping favorites, including "Love in the Hot Afternoon" and "Farewell Party." But cool or wet weather could wreak havoc on these outdoor concerts, cutting attendance and profits. This was just another reminder that a much larger home—one that could host indoor dances and concerts—was sorely needed.

Fund-Raising for an Arena Raising

In 1982, after decades of yearning for a larger venue, ATCLS&R was offered the opportunity to lease 128 acres of Walter E. Long Municipal Park in northeast Austin from the City of Austin for 50 years at a nominal fee. The land and any improvements made to it were to be turned over to the city when the lease expired. City voters first had to approve the lease. Show boosters used public presentations, outreach to the news media, and one-on-one meetings and letters courting community leaders to educate the public about its mission and to explain the need for a new facility. Their efforts paid off. Eighty percent of voting Austinites approved the lease on April 2, 1983, during the same election that pitted former sidewalk flower salesman Max Nofziger against Lowell Lebermann and Ron Mullen in a race to become Austin's next mayor.

With a site for the new venue confirmed, the group moved quickly forward by setting a daunting goal to construct a new main arena, a livestock barn and show arena, and a banquet hall in time to host its 1984 events. The

Program cover of the 1983 event. (Courtesy Star of Texas Fair and Rodeo)

AUSTIN–TRAVIS COUNTY
LIVESTOCK SHOW &
RODEO

MARCH 18-27

CITY COLISEUM

facility would serve the ATCLS&R a few weeks each year. The rest of the time, it would provide a needed new meeting and exhibit space for other groups.

But before serious fund-raising to finance construction could begin, the organization had to break from the chamber and incorporate as a nonprofit, tax-exempt entity. After more than 30 years of close association, the show and chamber parted ways amicably. In 1983, the group quickly incorporated and received approval for tax-exempt status with the help of U.S. Representative Jake Pickle. "Jimmy Callahan and I got on an airplane [to Dallas] after Jake Pickle made a phone call to the person who needed to approve it. He said it generally takes six months to do this. Within a week we had our 501(c)(3) status," Knolle said. "Jake was very supportive of the entire community, but he really helped our organization."

Now officially a charity, the show launched a major fund-raising effort in 1983 to build upon the seed money that had accumulated in the Louis J. Luedecke trust. Lifetime ATCLS&R memberships were offered for the first time. A charter lifetime member could join for $100, and by the time the 1983 show program went to print, 150 lifetime members had signed up.

"One of the first things we did was to organize a Founders Club," said Knolle, who was president at the time. The minimum contribution for this group, whose members received VIP treatment at show events, was $10,000 to be paid over five years. Knolle recalled that many contributors in that initial group donated much more than that. By February 1984, more

than 180 individuals had joined the club's rolls. Among other privileges, Founders Club members received an option to purchase box seats in the new rodeo arena and automatically became charter members of the exclusive Founders Club facility built on the third floor overlooking the arena. To this day, the club provides a restaurant, bar, and meeting space for its members.

The city's economic engine was chugging along during this time. Austin's unemployment rate had dropped to a three-year low of 2.8 percent, and commercial construction was running at a brisk pace, with a number of multi-million-dollar apartments, condominiums, offices, and warehouse projects permitted during the early part of 1984. Many area residents and companies were riding this wave of economic prosperity and gave generously to the construction project, donating money, labor, and materials. "We ended up with four and a half million dollars in pledges and cash donations and probably another two million to two and a half million dollars in in-kind donations," said Knolle. "The construction industry was doing very well, and the construction community really donated a large part of the funds, the work, and the materials in kind. Without that help we couldn't have done it."

Work was already under way on the construction site, which Knolle recalled was infested with rattlesnakes, when an official groundbreaking ceremony was held on October 5, 1983. Jimmy Callahan, the volunteer board member in charge of the new facility's construction, had begun organizing daily work parties. These crews, sometimes numbering hundreds of people on the weekends—including parents working alongside their children—pitched in throughout the fall and winter of 1983–84 in a race against the clock.

"There were several weekends that some of the cranes moved from [building projects] downtown to out here," recalled Mike Eledge, show president in 1986. "Two weekends in a row nearly every major piece of equipment was moved out here because of the ability we had to get people and stuff done. It was amazing. We built these parking lots in about four days. We had eighty, three-yard dump trucks working twenty-four hours a day. The trucks were donated, the gravel was donated by the Platt family of Hornsby Bend, and a lot of the drivers were giving their time because they cared." In the chamber's March 1984 issue of *Austin* magazine, the show's board expressed thanks to 1,500 volunteers and more than 35 businesses

for their "support and cooperation" during the facility's construction.

Dubbed the Texas Exposition and Heritage Center, the new facility was slated to officially open March 31, 1984, to host ATCLS&R's annual events for the first time. This meant work on the 7,000-seat main rodeo arena (with its 270-foot clear-span construction), the 120,000-square-foot covered livestock barns and show arena, and the 20,000-square-foot banquet hall (that could host up to 2,000 guests) could tolerate no bureaucratic delays. "We got great support from all the governmental officials. They bent over backwards to get us our building permits," Knolle recalled. Nonetheless, organizers planned two shows as the March 31 date approached—one in the Expo Center and the other in the City Coliseum—just in case the work was not finished in time.

The Luedecke Arena under construction in 1984 at the Texas Exposition and Heritage Center (now the Travis County Exposition Center). (Courtesy Austin American-Statesman/Jay Godwin)

Gala with Willie Nelson Christens Texas Exposition and Heritage Center

Volunteers scrambled to lay flooring, install seats, paint, and put in landscaping up until the last minute in March, with more still to do. But the fallback plan to use the City Coliseum was unnecessary. The group's 500 Club held the first-ever event in the newly constructed main arena on March 24, 1984. The club threw a steak dinner and party for more than 400 members and their families that night—a warm-up for the glamorous christening to come.

On the evening of March 30, more than 2,000 partiers, decked out in tuxes, boots, and formal Western wear, poured into the arena for the first gala ATCLS&R had ever held. Willie Nelson headlined the show, and tickets went for a hefty $100 apiece, a substantial price at that time. Sales from both a silent auction and a live auction—featuring everything from Western art and sets of autographed James Michener novels to top-of-their-breed quarter horses and cattle

(including an animal donated by Nelson)—went toward paying off the facility's construction bills. Tables were arranged on the main arena floor, which volunteers had covered the night before with garish green AstroTurf. Guests sipped cocktails and dined on a sumptuous buffet provided by well-known San Antonio caterer Don Strange. Celebrities who joined the organization's usual supporters that evening included actor James Garner, University of Texas at Austin alumnus and Houston Oilers running back Earl Campbell, and author Michener himself.

"We needed to have a fund-raiser to put ourselves on the map, and at that time Willie was about as big a name as there was in music," said Eledge. University of Texas at Austin's football coach Darrell Royal had pulled strings to get Knolle and Eledge an audience with the "Red-Headed Stranger" several months earlier so they could solicit his performance. The two met with Willie in his tour bus, which was parked outside the Austin Opry House on Austin's Academy Drive. Nelson was there preparing for a show. "We had a beer or two with him and explained what we were doing," Knolle said. "Willie said, 'Call my agent.'" Snagging Nelson as the featured entertainer and securing high-dollar items for the auction were crucial. "It was the first really big gala of its time in Austin," Knolle said. "The food was lavish. The live auction brought in excess of $200,000."

The next night, for the kickoff rodeo and concert by country star Don Williams, the saying "Build it and they will come," proved correct. "We were standing on the balcony, and it was headlights as far as you could see down Loyola and both ways down Decker Lane," Evans said. Volunteers at the gates were collecting $2 per car for parking but couldn't keep up with the deluge. "We were totally overwhelmed," Knolle said. "I'll never forget having a session the following morning to decide how to do it better. Somehow we managed to improve." An admission fee of $1 was charged to enter the grounds, but patrons could enter free as often as they liked by wearing a "Kicker Badge," which cost $2 and could be purchased from the chamber, Safeway, Callahan's General Store, and other retail outlets.

Crowds continued to throng onto the grounds for more than a week to enjoy the Mighty Thomas Carnival, a horseshoe tournament, and the children's barnyard. They also

Program cover from the 1984 event, the first held in the new Expo Center. (Courtesy Star of Texas Fair and Rodeo)

packed the arena for eight more nights of rodeo, produced by Lester Meier, and musical entertainment provided by national stars such as Reba McEntire, Bobby Bare, and Tammy Wynette. The few remaining reserved box seats sold for $7 each. Reserved seating on the mezzanine was $6, and reserved upper-level seats were $3 each during the week and $5 on Friday through Sunday.

The rodeo again included a calf scramble as part of the evening festivities. A scramble had been part of the organization's annual events

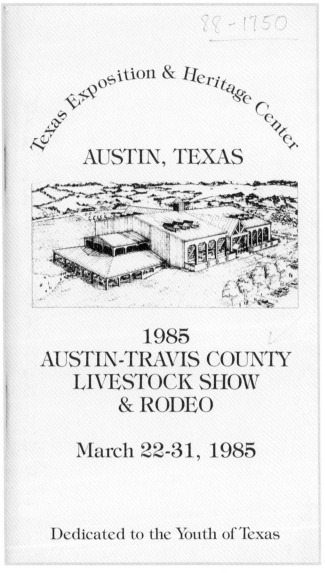

Program cover from the 1985 event. (Courtesy Star of Texas Fair and Rodeo)

as early as 1949 but had not been held in several years. Forty-five of the youths participating received certificates for $500 to purchase heifers they were expected to enter in the following year's livestock show.

Even though finishing touches were still needed on the buildings and grounds, show organizers settled into their new home. The banquet hall alone served multiple purposes and accommodated almost twice as many youth fair entries as had Palmer Auditorium the previous year—980 rather than 500. It also hosted an art show, the poultry and rabbit judging, and the livestock auction. The new livestock barn and show arena welcomed 1,838 livestock and horse show entries that first year.

The grand champion steer in 1984 brought $21,000 for contestant Jon Bishop of Austin—the highest price paid so far at the annual auction. Auction receipts increased to a record $656,000; a year earlier they had been $439,000. About 800 bidders and spectators attended the auction, during which 28 steers, 64 lambs, 75 hogs, 20 turkeys, 50 capons, 20 pens of rabbits, and 40 pens of broilers were sold. The youth fair auction brought a total of $54,000 in sales that year, more than double the previous year's take.

Despite the parking snarl and minor plumbing and electrical problems, the inaugural events in the new venue were a resounding success. The *Austin American-Statesman* reported that the rodeo drew an average nightly attendance of 6,000 and sold out four nights. In a letter to Robert Sneed dated May 16, 1984, Texas Governor Mark White couldn't have better

CHAPTER 4

summarized the organization's recent accomplishments: "Congratulations on the outstanding success of the Austin Travis County Livestock Show. Your new facility is outstanding, and the fashion in which you brought it about was exemplary."

During the next five years the organization continued to innovate and expand its programs and activities as it made the most of its new, larger home. A fact sheet compiled by the show notes a number of milestones during this era; in 1985 those included the first "pen of three" commercial replacement heifer show and sale, in which 125 heifers grossed $172,225; and an expanded calf scramble that included 108 participants, who took home $37,800 in calf purchase certificates.

The following year the group hosted its first barn dance and welcomed 2,500 children touring its children's barnyard. Also that year, the rodeo parade became one of the state's major events celebrating the Texas Sesquicentennial. Notable activities in 1987 included a junior consumer decision-making contest, a public-speaking contest, and fashion show, as well as a youth dance, baby boomer's dance, and a chili cook-off. A heritage classic heifer show for Travis County entrants and a special market steer program were held in 1988, and a princess contest was established for girls under 19.

The rodeo took a huge leap forward in 1989 when the Professional Rodeo Cowboys Association (PRCA) sanctioned it. Bradford Ivy and Mike Cervi produced the professional sporting event, which featured about 475 professional cowboys that first year.

Expo Center Goes to Travis County

The 1980s were full of major accomplishments for the organization, but the latter half of that decade was also marked by financial strain. Shortly after moving into the Expo Center, show leaders began to realize they faced a daunting challenge—especially for a primarily volunteer-run organization. They were responsible for the huge task of year-round facility maintenance and the marketing and booking of the Expo Center during the 11 months of the year when they were not putting on their own events. "We had a tiger by the tail," Eledge said. "We couldn't rent it for close to what it cost to operate it."

Furthermore, in the late 1980s the savings and loan crisis and a nationwide recession pulled Austin's economy down. "Times were horrible," said Tommy Carlson, show president in 1988, who recalled having to lay off more than 100 employees in his engineering business at the time. Donor pledges stopped coming in when the economy went south, Carlson said, so the organization had trouble making payments on loans it had taken out as construction bills mounted.

"We lost a lot of the pledges because [businesses] just weren't producing or they had gone into bankruptcy," Knolle said. "As a result, we weren't able to service the debt to pay the construction price that we had incurred. We started shopping for ways to salvage the transaction." The banks renegotiated the notes and gave the organization extensions on making payments. "The banks stuck with us," Carlson recalled.

"We knew our local bankers. They helped us tremendously." At one point a number of show leaders even co-signed on the construction loans. "At the time that we offered the personal guarantees, it was a way of getting a further extension and giving us some time to pursue other options," Knolle said. "We didn't want to let a lot of people down. A number of us felt strongly enough about the mission that we were willing to do that."

Local government entities were also of assistance. The Austin City Council had already helped by providing financing to help pay Expo Center construction costs. In March 1985, it voted to issue $4.5 million in tax-exempt revenue bonds, after holding a public hearing during which no one spoke in opposition. Travis County in 1987 supported the show with $325,000 in county funds, according to county records. "It's the only thing that got us through that next year," Carlson said. But, he said, he got the impression the county would soon be discontinuing its annual support.

Knolle said he and others approached several wealthy individuals as well as the Travis County Commissioners to seek a buyer for the facility. The county was interested. According to Commissioners Court minutes from December 7, 1988, commissioners approved the issuance of $3.5 million in certificates of obligation to acquire the Expo Center from the ATCLS&R. The purchase was finalized in June 1989. "The banks were all for it," Carlson said. "They got some of their money back. The county got a heck of a deal." Mike Levi, president in 1990, said it was a relief once Travis County took over the Expo Center. "We were trying to stay afloat at that time," Levi recalled. "It got us out from under this thing that was dragging us down each year."

The passion, hard work, and generosity of hundreds of people, including many entire families, had gone into building the Expo Center. Philanthropist Louis J. Luedecke's name, emblazoned on the main arena, reminded the group how long it had been working toward this goal. "We had all put our hearts and souls into this place. To sell it was a difficult transition, but it was something that needed to be done because we were in the business of giving money to kids, not operating a facility," said Linda Raven, a longtime ATCLS&R volunteer and staff member who served as executive director from 1990 through the 2000 show.

In many ways, turning its "baby" over to Travis County wasn't easy. But once relieved of this financial burden, the ATCLS&R was able to stabilize its operations, further develop its programs, and reach new heights in the years to come. ❧

1938-1988

APRIL 8-17, 1988

TEXAS EXPOSITION
& HERITAGE CENTER

AUSTIN, TEXAS

Commemorative Poster Sponsored by KSSR Country 107 FM
© 1988 Phinney-Stacey & Associates Inc., Illustration & Design Randy Phinney

Poster from the 1988 event. (Courtesy Jeff Nash)

PARADES BROUGHT WESTERN HERITAGE TO CAPITAL CITY

For years, Western heritage displays enlivened Austin's Congress Avenue and heralded the start of the annual livestock show and rodeo in a procession of marching bands, horseback riders, national stars, and local heroes.

Under sunny skies and blessed by 70-degree weather on March 3, 1952, city dwellers lined Congress Avenue to watch a blocks-long cavalcade of cowboys on horseback, marching bands, and mounted Texas Rangers in the first parade held to kick off the Capital Area Livestock Show and junior rodeo. The Bergstrom Air Force Base Band led the mile-long march, followed immediately by cowboy singer and Western movie star Tex Ritter. A contingent of mounted Texas Rangers accompanied Ritter, who sat atop his horse, White Flash.

The Capital Area Farm and Ranch Club, which ran the livestock show from 1950 to 1956, staged only a handful of parades, but it made sure they were doozies. The 1954 procession featured silver-screen cowboy Johnny Mack Brown, clad in blue and cream Western wear and sporting a 10-gallon hat. The procession took more than an hour to wind its way from the State Capitol to the City Coliseum, according to the *Austin Statesman*.

Parade participants competed for prizes in 1955 for best band, best commercial float, best mounted organization, and best horse-drawn vehicle. The next year, the Capital Area Farm and Ranch Club felt hard times and canceled the junior rodeo, reduced the size of the livestock show, and held the parade one last time. During that last march, Dave Shanks, agricultural editor for the Austin dailies, reported that

the El Campo Spanish Trail Riders were due to arrive in Austin in time to join the parade, making this 1956 trail ride perhaps the first to be associated with the livestock show.

Not until 1979, during the Austin Chamber of Commerce's sponsorship of the ATCLS&R, did a parade again became part of the annual festivities. For the first few years, no motorized vehicles were allowed. "Frank Newsom was responsible for starting the nonmotorized parade," said Ted Nagel, ATCLS&R president in 1981. "We'd sometimes have as many as seventy units—all on horseback or pulled by wagons."

VIPs and the parade announcer perched on the balcony of the Stephen F. Austin Hotel at Seventh Street overlooking Congress Avenue. Nagel recalled in the early 1980s that his wife, Harriet, would hurriedly type up the list of participants for the announcer in order of their appearance as they assembled outside the City Coliseum. "She'd be down in the chamber office madly writing up the script, and the National Guard would put her in a jeep and take her to the Stephen F. Austin before the parade started," Nagel said.

The 1980 procession included everyone from Lieutenant Governor Bill Hobby Jr., the Travis County Commissioners, and the Austin City Council to the Lanier High School Drill Team, the Austin Police Rodeo Team, and the Williamson County Sheriff's Posse.

By 1986, the livestock show's volunteer crew was seasoned at staging parades. It joined forces with the City of Austin and state efforts to celebrate Texas' 150th birthday in Austin by co-producing a Texas Sesquicentennial event

that was the largest procession the city had seen, recalled Mike Eledge, who served as board president that year. "It was televised in eleven cities," he noted. "This was the second-biggest event—next to the 1984 gala with Willie Nelson—that our organization had staged. It really gave us a lot of credibility and publicity for the new facility."

Everything went smoothly that year until parade participants finishing the route could not get into the two state parking lots east of the Capitol that were supposed to be the destaging area, recalled Haskell Griffin, who served on the Parade Committee at the time and became board president in 1996. Entrances to the lots were blocked by traffic because a miscommunication with police meant the area had not been cordoned off, said Griffin. The ensuing congestion threatened to bring the entire procession to a halt. He and others quickly used several vehicles to stop traffic near the parking lots and ushered parade units off the street as rapidly as possible.

"We shut down central Austin," said Griffin, laughing. "The police showed up and said, 'You can't do this' and 'You need to move that truck.' I said, 'Well, it won't start.' The officer laughed and said, 'Well, you're going to be finished by the time I can do anything about it.'"

The livestock show continued to hold its annual parade through the 1980s and 1990s.

The 1987 event, led by Grand Marshall Jody Conradt, Texas Lady Longhorns head basketball coach, was broadcast live on KTBC-TV. About a decade later, in 1996, the ATCLS&R's cowboy breakfast kicked off the procession. Early-rising spectators were treated to breakfast tacos, biscuits and sausage, and steaming cups of coffee at Eleventh Street and Congress Avenue before that year's cavalcade headed south down Congress at 10:00 a.m.

The charity held the last of its parades in the early 2000s. Twenty-first-century downtown Austin, with its multistoried, glass-walled office buildings, presented a very different setting for the event than the view Tex Ritter scanned in 1952 from horseback. But one spot along the route had not changed much throughout the organization's parade years— the southwest corner of Eleventh Street and Congress Avenue. The historic, temporary State Capitol grounds, home to Austin's first Baby Beef Show in 1940, continued to be a reminder of the charity's humble origins in the heart of Texas' capital city.

Roughly half a century after Austin Chamber of Commerce leaders held Austin's first Baby Beef Show, Travis County included considerably less land under the plow and hoof. The county had 514,276 agricultural acres in 1940 but only 332,826 in 1992. The county's 4-H and FFA youth continued to show animals as children had done in the decades before them. Many proudly took home ribbons, buckles, and cash prizes or walked away with checks after the annual auction of their winning steers, lambs, hogs, turkeys, rabbits, broilers, and capons. Show entries dropped over the decade, from 848 in 1990 to 500 in 1999, perhaps because of Travis County's increasing urbanization.

In 1990, the Austin area was still recovering from the recession from the end of the previous decade, and the auction's gross sales—$197,803—reflected that. The grand champion steer raised by Jason Weiss of Richland sold that year for $9,175 to Sirloin Stockade and 1990 show president Mike Levi.

As the economy improved, so did sales. Receipts increased more than threefold to gross $485,286 in 1995. Randall Hees of Pflugerville walked away with a record $27,500 check from Mike McCarty for his 1,218-pound grand champion steer—the highest premium ever paid in the show's history at that time. Hees was one in a long line of Hees family members who had taken home grand champion or reserve champion honors throughout the history of the show.

A new record came in 1999 when Brandy Murchison, also of Pflugerville, earned $70,000 for her grand champion steer, which was purchased by Richard Wallrath, owner of Champion Window in New Braunfels. Levi recalls during that decade, "We were by far the largest, most successful county show in the state."

As in earlier years, the prizes and money many show winners earned through the competition and youth livestock auction were important, but the education all participants received through their experience remained invaluable. They not only learned how to care for and show their animals but also how to achieve goals through hard work and responsibility. Stan Voelker, the volunteer in charge of the Livestock Show Committee during much of the 1990s, recalls many children showing year after year: "It was a super rewarding time watching the kids grow up and come through," said Voelker, who served as show president in 1999. "Some would start as early as third grade and end up showing until they were seniors."

When Shelley Talley and her older sister, Becky Silco, each turned nine, they began participating in the Austin–Travis County Livestock Show. Each year until their graduation from Pflugerville High School—in 2000 and 1996, respectively—the girls competed with pigs, steers, lambs, rabbits, or turkeys. This decade of caring for and showing animals taught them to assume responsibility, have determination, and take pride in their efforts. "These projects are seven days a week no matter what you have planned or the weather," Talley said. "You learn to take pride in yourself and your animal, and that in turn carries over into your work life and personal life." Talley recalled meeting people from all walks of life at the shows, making connections that later led to her obtaining a degree in animal science from San Angelo State University. "You have no idea the networking you can do and the lifelong friends you make."

Now a mother, Silco is proud of what her oldest son, who has competed with steers for eight years, has accomplished and learned. "I have two more children coming up to be show age and am looking forward to many more

Nine-year-old Mindy Morrow waits with her bunnies for judging to begin during the 1991 show. (Courtesy Austin American-Statesman/ *Karen Warren)*

years in show barns and seeing the oldest pass his knowledge down to them," Silco said. "The combination of responsibility you develop along with the confidence and lifelong contacts you make through livestock show participation cannot be denied or replaced."

Planning, Logistics Improve Income

In 1995, ATCLS&R president Curtis Calhoun, a trusted Austin businessman and certified public accountant, brought improved fiscal responsibility to the organization when he took a scrupulous look at its finances and developed a financial oversight plan of action. The plan was needed for the busy charity, whose volunteers had their hands full. By the mid-1990s, ATCLS&R had under its belt a decade of experience staging a rodeo, livestock show, and auction; a youth fair and auction; a carnival; a barbecue cook-off; and a multitude of other annual events at what was by now called the Travis County Exposition Center.

In 1995, the first cowboy breakfast was held as part of the charity's annual kickoff events. Volunteers cooked and served 5,400 eggs, 200 pounds of bacon, 175 pounds of cheese, and 5,000 tortillas to crowds in the Highland Mall parking lot. Motorola sponsored this first early-morning fete.

The ProRodeo, which as of 1989 had been sanctioned by the Professional Rodeo Cowboys Association, was attracting crowds to watch exciting riding and roping events featuring top professional cowboys and cowgirls, includ-

Governor George Bush and a livestock show supporter pose during a cowboy breakfast on Auditorium Shores in the late 1990s. (Courtesy Linda Raven)

ing World Champion All-Around Cowboy Ty Murray and World Champion Bull Rider Tuff Hedeman. Crowds also came for the concerts held in conjunction with the rodeo, which featured nationally known performers such as Ricky Van Shelton, Rick Trevino, and George Jones.

Carnivals staged by Bill Hames Shows, Ray Cammack Shows, and Alamo Midway thrilled fairgoers during the 1990s. Children and their families could also count on a number of attractions to entertain and educate them during this decade, including a petting zoo, a mobile dairy classroom, and armadillo and pig races.

Through the mid-1990s the thousands arriving daily at the Expo Center for these and other attractions had been able to park wherever they desired once they paid a parking fee and drove through the center's gate. Members of the organization's volunteer committees and their crews (and anyone else who arrived early enough) often claimed the choice parking spaces. Cars crowded chock-a-block around the show barn and other buildings, sometimes parked five rows deep. "This caused chaos, especially if someone needed to get out," recalled Haskell Griffin, show president in 1996.

Other show logistics needed fixing. The area on the south side of the Luedecke Arena that could have been leased to commercial exhibitors was instead being use for parking by volunteers and was difficult for pedestrians to access. In addition, patrons didn't pay a fee to enter the fairgrounds. Sources of potential income weren't being tapped, Griffin said. "We were in one of those things where income had leveled off and expenses kept going up and up and up and up," he added. "So everybody kind of knew that we needed a change."

The solution was a board-approved plan for the 1996 show that restricted parking to designated areas and made former parking space around Expo facilities off limits. Griffin recalled that even with the plan in place it was still hard to get committee members to give up their parking perks. "We basically went from a culture of [committees] having free rein to them starting to be given guidelines and expected to follow those and coordinate with other parts of the show," he said.

In its first year at the Expo Center, 1984, the ATCLS&R charged a $1-per-person entry fee and collected parking fees from drivers, but the charity had not been charging an admission fee since then. In 1996, the board decided to make a change. "That was quite a debate," Griffin said. Admission that year was $2 per head, but children 12 and under could enter free. Terrell Hamann, who had been president in 1993, built the turnstiles and portals that defined the show's first entry gates.

That same year a pedestrian bridge, designed by Tommy Carlson, who had been show president in 1988, and built by Capital Excavation Company for a discounted price, connected the area north of the Luedecke Arena with the area to its south. "In 1996, our show took a big step forward. By building the bridge, we opened up the whole south side [outside] of the arena to sell to commercial exhibitors, which we did," Griffin said. "It was finished about one week before the show. It started the flow of pedestrian traffic from the north to the south."

Griffin said a new Logistics Committee, headed by Hamann and that included Voelker; Jeff Nash, president in 1994; and Jim Achilles, who became president in 1997, handled these new details in time to put on the show. He also credited Linda Raven, the show's executive director during this decade, for her leadership throughout the changes. "She was the guiding light that lit our way," he said.

All in all, the innovations resulted in more income. "I think we netted over $300,000 that year," Griffin said. Charging a fairgrounds admission fee and booting committee members off their favorite parking spots may have been controversial issues to tackle, but these were minor compared to what leaders took on next.

"We had a huge county show," Voelker said. "That led us to believe that we had the infrastructure to take it to the next level." Although it was a large county show, the number of Travis County youth participating had decreased and the amount raised by livestock auction sales had declined along with it. During his presidency, Voelker, Raven, and others proposed to the ATCLS&R's 50-plus-member board that—starting in 2000—the group hold a regional show for 4-H and FFA youth in Bastrop, Blanco, Burnet, Caldwell, Hays, Lee, Williamson, and Travis counties in March in addition to staging the Travis County youth show in January.

Raven said it was a fight to expand the show beyond the borders of Travis County. "It was a struggle because you had so many people who for so long had gone this way [Travis County only]," Raven said. "The [local] ag world had this fabulous resource all to themselves for a long time, so the thought of having to share it with other counties was a difficult sell." Voelker said even he had once been opposed to the idea until Raven helped change his mind. Leaders had discussed the topic since at least the mid-1990s, but it was a challenge to convince some board members of its merit. Raven recalled that some leaders were happy with continuing to hold a countywide youth show, but "I saw it so much bigger and grander. We had a responsibility to do it—being the capital city. We had enough money," she said. "We had the grounds and the space."

Equally challenging was convincing the agriculture teachers, county agricultural extension agents, county commissioners, and the parents of 4-H and FFA youth to buy in to the ATCLS&R's plans. Many feared the show's expansion would hurt the chances of their county's kids winning show prizes and earning money from livestock sales, Voelker said. ATCLS&R representatives traveled the region to meet with concerned residents and community leaders to ease their fears and encourage regional businesses to participate by bidding at the livestock auction. "[We wanted] to try to convince them that we had the infrastructure set up that we weren't going to take any money away from their kids," Voelker said.

On September 23, 1998, the ATCLS&R board met to cast their votes. According to board minutes, President-elect Donnie Williams reported that based on the findings of the Regional Show Committee created to study the issue, it was in the best interests of the show to expand beyond Travis County to the seven adjacent counties. He pointed out that the population in the region had grown so much that the Austin area was now considered to include most of the seven counties. He also argued that reaching out to these counties to include them in the show would encourage participation at the livestock auction by bidders from these communities, helping to boost decreasing auction receipts.

After lengthy discussion about the pros and cons of going regional, the board made the landmark decision—in a vote of 39 to 9—in favor. This momentous change propelled the ATCLS&R on a path of expansion into the twenty-first century with an aim to rival the major livestock shows in San Antonio, Fort Worth, and Houston. 🐎

PRORODEO EVOLVED FROM CALF SCRAMBLES IN 1949

The annual 15-night Rodeo Austin performances have become one of Austin's most popular March attractions, and they pour thousands of dollars into the Star of Texas Fair and Rodeo's charity coffers. But much like the organization's livestock show, this ProRodeo has humble beginnings that aren't so well known.

Early Rodeo-Type Competitions

The first rodeo-type events scheduled in conjunction with the livestock show appear to have been two calf scrambles held in 1949. One was held for 4-H Club boys, and the other, for three Travis County FFA chapters. The competitions were held in the Travis County Junior Livestock Show's new venue—the City Coliseum. Boys who corralled calves were expected to exhibit the fattened animals at next year's show. Calves were donated by local businessmen, including Fred Catterall of Walker Austex Chili Company, Taylor Glass of Polar Ice Cream Company, and E. A. Moeller of Superior Dairies.

Boys on foot attempted to snare calves quickly in calf roping and throwing exhibitions, added in 1950. A calf scramble sponsored by the Austin American-Statesman company and a greased pig scramble were also held that year. It appears that this was the first year music became part of the nighttime roundups, with the Austin Junior High and Austin High School bands performing during the two-night show.

First Junior Rodeo

When calf riding was added to the competition roster in 1951, farm-and-ranch editor Dave Shanks's pre-event coverage in the *Austin Statesman* announced, "Junior Rodeo Opens Tuesday with Greased Pig Scramble." This first official junior rodeo held in association with the livestock show featured about 100 boys from Austin and area high schools competing during March 4, 5, and 6.

The Capital Area Farm and Ranch Club, which put on the livestock show and rodeo at this time, pulled out all the stops in 1952. The organizers added a pig scramble and cow-milking contests for girls to help round out a program of what had been boys-only events. Livestock judge Jack Miller selected the grand champion steer, shown by Elgin FFA student Curtis Neidig, as a highlight during the second rodeo performance. Audience members, who packed the Coliseum stands, paid $3.00 for reserved seats and $1.80 for general admission. Kids got in for $0.75.

Excitement built each evening during the event as the dust settled and the featured attraction—Tex Ritter—entered the arena. The nationally known country-music singer and Western movie actor grew up in East Texas and had attended the University of Texas Law School for a year. Night upon night, Ritter and his band entertained the crowd with songs such as "Boll Weevil," "Blood on the Saddle," and "Rye Whisky." Country singer and songwriter Merle Travis and his band shared the spotlight and performed "Divorce Me C.O.D." and other Travis favorites. Glenn and Tip, border collies from the Peterson Ranch in Kerrville, completed the show, which master of ceremonies and KTBC radio personality Cactus Pryor kept moving with his homespun humor.

In 1953, the nightly rodeo featured 150 contestants and a show that starred the Duke of Paducah, a Grand Ole Opry comedian and banjo player. Martha Lynn of Austin also wowed the crowd with her trick horseback riding. For the first time, the rodeo in 1954 crowned a queen, Janice Germany of Burnet.

The next year, the rodeo had expanded to include calf roping, bareback bronc riding, steer riding, a cloverleaf barrel race for cowgirls, and a boy-girl team ribbon roping contest. According to newspaper and chamber accounts of the 1950s, the final junior rodeo was held in 1955, although youth events such as calf and pig scrambles and goat sacking and roping competitions were held from the late 1950s through the 1960s.

Amateur Rodeo Begins

The City Coliseum arena was a restricted venue for holding such events and could seat only about 2,000, but show leaders expanded the competitions by the end of the 1960s. In March 1969, the chamber announced in its *Austin* magazine that Cecil Hill of Oak Hill would provide stock for a three-night rodeo to be held in conjunction with the livestock show that year. It was an amateur rodeo, although some accounts incorrectly labeled it "professional." Tickets were $0.75 for children and $1.25 for adults. The next year the rodeo expanded to five performances, including two matinees. Contests included bronc riding, calf roping, bull dogging, barrel racing, and bull riding. With rodeos now becoming an important part of its assorted events, the Austin Livestock Show appropriately became known as the Austin Livestock Show and Rodeo (ALS&R) in 1970.

After the rodeo started up again in 1969, concerts were slated during rodeo intermissions, said Lynn Griffin, who was Austin Chamber of Commerce agricultural manager at the time. Country-and-western music star Johnny Rodriguez, a Sabinal, Texas, native, performed three times at the 1973 event. Verlin Callahan, president in 1973, booked Rodriguez after he heard him singing in English and Spanish on the radio and knew the performer would be a hit with the rodeo crowd. Rodriguez had won the Most Promising Male Vocalist award from the Academy of Country Music in 1972. Callahan called Arlie Duff, a DJ with KVET, who gave him the name of Rodriguez's promoter, Happy Shahan. "We didn't have a stage or anything," said Callahan. "So we put four risers out in the middle of the arena. He didn't have a band, so we hired a fiddle player for him. We gave him $1,000 for three appearances."

The following year, in 1974, country singers Sammi Smith and Bob Luman performed each night during the rodeo intermission. Smith was known for recording Kris Kristofferson's "Help Me Make It through the Night," and Luman had a hit with "Lonely Women Make Good Lovers." Tickets to the combined rodeo and concert were $3.00 in advance and $3.50 at the door.

The City Coliseum provided an intimate setting for the concerts and an exciting venue for rodeo contestants and fans. Jay Evans, who

Cecil Hill (third from right) with crew members of the Cecil Hill Rodeo Company, which produced the rodeo for many years starting in 1969. Back row (from left to right), Donald Bell, Bobby Joe Bartley, Lester Shiller, Alford Hill, Don Shiller, Billy Shiller; and front, Sidney Pruitt. (Courtesy Carolyn and Alford Hill)

served as livestock show president in 1979 and 1985, experienced the small Coliseum arena firsthand roping steers during the 1973 and 1974 rodeos. He said because of the limited space, rodeo producers set up events dif-ferently. Animals to be roped weren't given a head start; instead, they were released at the same time the riders left the box. "The arena was probably one hundred feet long, maybe one hundred ten. I remember we ran the timed events diagonally [to give the contestants more room]," Evans said. "You were either ready to rope or you had *no time*."

Many rodeo fans—seated only a few feet from the action—were close enough to hear the snort of a bucking bull or to be pelted by dirt kicked up by a sprinting horse. "There was a lot of crowd interaction. The front-row seats were ground level [with the contestants]. The first row was stirrup high," Evans said. "We didn't have a wall; we had chain link fencing" between fans and the cowboys. "I'm amazed no one was hurt."

Hill produced the rodeo until 1978 when Lester Meier of Fredericksburg took it over, said Evans. By 1979 the chamber reported that the five-night rodeo attracted more than 800 contestants. Meier recalled that at that time the annual event was considered an "open pro rodeo" in which amateur and professional cowboys and cowgirls competed against each other. "The attitude was if it's fair for one, it's fair for all." As many as 1,000 contestants participated annually. Because there were so many contestants, not all could be scheduled during the evening performances. They got their time in the arena during "slack," which was scheduled in the afternoons, a common feature at rodeos. "We had all the world champion guys entering, like calf roper Joe Beaver of Huntsville, team roper Tee Wolman of Llano, and bull rider Ronnie Witfield of Houston," Meier recalled. In

Rodeo producer Cecil Hill, Austin Chamber of Commerce Agricultural Secretary Lynn Griffin, and country singer Johnny Rodriguez (standing second, third, and fourth from left) pose with three unidentified men. Rodriguez performed during the 1973 rodeo. (Courtesy Carolyn and Alford Hill)

Rodeo clowns/bullfighters Dave
Garrison, Alford Hill, and Lester
Shiller pose during a performance in
the 1970s. (Courtesy Carolyn and
Alford Hill)

A bareback rider competes at the 1977
Austin Livestock Show and Rodeo.
(Courtesy Carolyn and Alford Hill)

Bull rider Bubba Morrison competes
in 1977. (Courtesy Carolyn and
Alford Hill)

Hollida

addition, for a few years an Old Timers Rodeo for contestants 40 years and older was added to the schedule on Sunday afternoons, Meier said.

Evans and Meier remembered an exciting night at the rodeo in the late 1970s. A bull penned behind the Coliseum got loose and trotted off between the carnival rides and Bouldin Creek, headed for Barton Springs Road. "Everybody saw it happen," Evans recalled. "Darwin Harrison was arriving for the team roping event that night, and he was stopped at the light at First Street and Barton Springs Road when he saw the bull coming toward them," Meier said. "He and a couple other cowboys unloaded their horses, got on them, and roped the bull. They loaded him into a trailer," Meier said. "It was a

crazy time. Thank God no one got hurt." The wandering bovine made the front page of the *Austin American-Statesman* the next morning.

Mike Eledge, president in 1986, was a volunteer assistant to the rodeo announcer for 21 years—from 1980 to 2000. He recalled that when the show was staged in the City Coliseum, he delivered last-minute information about lost children or new rodeo sponsors to the announcer by jotting the information on slips of paper and placing them in a paint bucket, which was hauled up to the announcer's stand by rope. "It was very unsophisticated," Eledge said, laughing.

By 1983, the last year the livestock show and rodeo were held in the Coliseum, contestants vied for over $20,000 in prize money. The ATCLS&R program that year called it "the largest indoor open rodeo in Texas."

Rodeo Moves to Expo Center, Goes Pro

After the ATCLS&R settled into its new home at the Texas Exposition and Heritage Center in March 1984, fans packed the Luedecke Arena during the nine-night rodeo. It was the first time calf roping, bareback riding, bull riding, barrel racing, and calf scramble competitions in Austin were held in such a large arena—210 feet long. Meier told the *Austin American-Statesman* at the time that steers and calves would have more room to run than in the City Coliseum, but the contestants would also have more room to jockey for the best position. Today, Meier recalled, "The first time we drove up and saw the new arena, we thought, 'this is like paradise.' The contestants loved it. It was breathtaking."

In 1989, the ATCLS&R stepped up the caliber of its competitions when the rodeo was sanctioned by the Professional Rodeo Cowboys Association. Starting that year, only professional cowboys and cowgirls who were PRCA members were allowed to compete. ATCLS&R also hired a new rodeo producer, Mike Cervi of Colorado. That year Cervi told a reporter he supplied the rodeo with 150 horses, 100 bulls, 100 steers, and 33 "pickup hands" who acted as technical assistants, stock handlers, bullfighters, and clowns. Cervi was assisted by Texas stock contractor Brad Ivy.

As word spread that the ATCLS&R now had a ProRodeo, dozens of world champion cowboys and cowgirls began to stop in Austin as they traveled the rodeo circuit. The event started to draw dozens of top-tier athletes, including World Champion All-Around Cowboy Ty Murray of Stephenville, Texas; World Champion Bull Rider Tuff Hedeman of Bowie, Texas; and World Champion Saddle Bronc Rider Billy Etbauer from Edmond, Oklahoma.

While these well-known world-class cowboys and cowgirls made the headlines, professionals at all levels ensured the fast-paced and often dangerous competitions went off without a hitch. Professional bullfighters who protected bull riders in the ATCLS&R's arena as early as the 1990s included Leon Coffee and Rick Chatman. Hadley Barrett, National ProRodeo Hall of Fame inductee and four-time PRCA Announcer of the Year, has presided over the shows since the 1990s as the master of ceremonies, announcing competitors, helping to keep the crowds entertained during lulls in the action, and recognizing sponsors.

During its first two decades as a ProRodeo, ATCLS&R's ticket sales and prize money for contestants grew. In 1990, rodeo ticket sales for 10 performances totaled about $350,000, setting a record for the ATCLS&R. Although there are no records of total rodeo ticket sales during the late 1990s, 80 percent of the seats were taken during the 13 rodeos staged in 1997.

George Strait is surrounded by fans after his performance at the 1985 Austin–Travis County Livestock Show and Rodeo; (left to right) Brenda Richter, Calley Callahan, Amy Callahan, Donna Higgins, and Jonelle Callahan. (Courtesy Calley Callahan Asklund)

The $10 ticket price in 1985 included entrance to the rodeo and a George Strait concert. (Courtesy Calley Callahan Asklund)

Country-western musician George Strait competes in team roping during the 1990 rodeo. (Courtesy Austin American-Statesman/ Ralph Barrera)

Rodeo Austin Moves
into the Twenty-first Century

From those early rodeos staged by the Travis County Junior Livestock Show during the 1950s to the show put on by the Star of Texas Fair and Rodeo today, musical entertainment has always been part of the bill. Not surprisingly, country-and-western performers have reigned supreme during most of the nightly rodeo concerts, including Willie Nelson, George Strait, Reba McEntire, Charlie Daniels, Tammy Wynette, and George Jones. In the 1980s and 1990s, the group began occasionally to deviate from the norm by booking rock, pop, Tejano, soul, and other non-country-and-western acts, such as La Mafia and the Temptations.

In 2001, the charity doubled its entertainment budget to bring in even bigger names and more diverse acts that would draw their fans through the doors, including those who might not otherwise attend a rodeo. The usual rodeo crowd favorites such as Toby Keith, Martina McBride, and Willie Nelson all appeared on concert bills, but so did rhythm-and-blues group Destiny's Child, soul legend James Brown, and rap star Nelly, whose performance set an arena attendance record in 2005. "We've tried to appeal to people of all walks of life," said Katy Blankinship, senior manager. "We want to be inclusive, not exclusive."

In 2010, music lovers filled every seat as well as the arena floor, setting a new arena record of 7,472 attendees for the band Lady Antebellum, which was chosen as top new group in 2009 by the Academy of Country Music.

"The magic is putting the two [rodeo and musical entertainment] together," Blankinship said. Beginning in 2001 the technical production of both the rodeo and nightly concerts was stepped up, as the charity hired professional crews to provide lighting, sound effects, and other special effects, such as lasers and pyrotechnics, to the nightly performances. Leading these efforts have been Tony Carey of LD Systems, who serves as chief of sound and light, and Howard Fletcher of First In Last Out Designs, who is in charge of stage production.

"I was told before I moved here that Austin is not a rodeo town," said Bucky Lamb, chief executive officer. "But the rodeo now is presented in a format that makes it more desirable. The very top competitors are coming here. Now, eight-time World Champion All-Around Cowboy Trevor Brazile headlines an all-star cast of ProRodeo athletes, including Fred Whitfield, Cody Ohl, J. W. Harris, and Will Lowe."

In the early 2000s, rodeo production was changed to ratchet up the excitement in the arena before the show and keep it going between competitions. That production style continues to this day. Hard-rock music booms as announcers tease the audience with details about the contestants and tough competitions to come.

The rodeo's opening few minutes is fast paced and gets attendees' hearts going with lasers, engaging video, a momentary blackout in the arena, and eardrum-thudding fireworks. "This isn't your grandpa's rodeo. It's slam open the chute and spur 'em for eight. It's edgy, Wild West action at its best. And it packs the grandstands!" Lamb said. "Ticket sales are at an all-time high."

Willie Nelson performing at Rodeo Austin in 2008. (Courtesy Star of Texas Fair and Rodeo)

Rap star Nelly performing in the Luedecke Arena in 2005. (Courtesy Star of Texas Fair and Rodeo)

A 2005 Rodeo Austin poster highlights the musicians scheduled nightly following the ProRodeo and Xtreme Bull Riding performances. (Courtesy Star of Texas Fair and Rodeo)

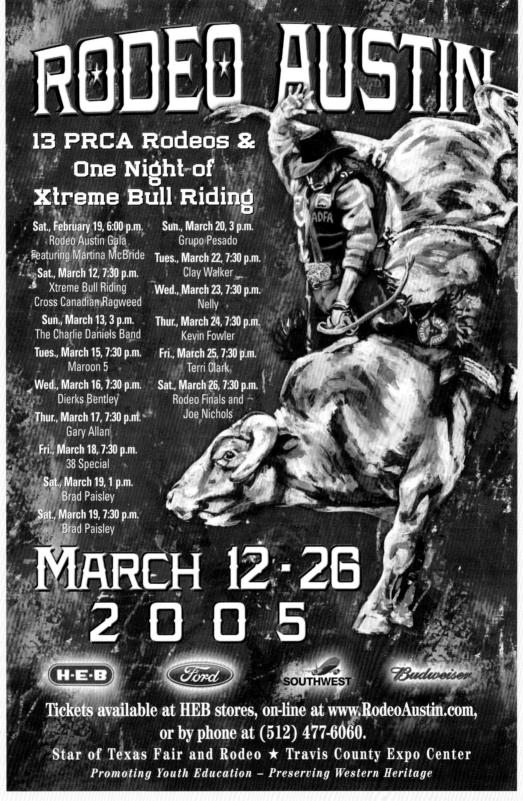

RODEO AUSTIN

13 PRCA Rodeos & One Night of Xtreme Bull Riding

Sat., February 19, 6:00 p.m.
Rodeo Austin Gala
Featuring Martina McBride

Sat., March 12, 7:30 p.m.
Xtreme Bull Riding
Cross Canadian Ragweed

Sun., March 13, 3 p.m.
The Charlie Daniels Band

Tues., March 15, 7:30 p.m.
Maroon 5

Wed., March 16, 7:30 p.m.
Dierks Bentley

Thur., March 17, 7:30 p.m.
Gary Allan

Fri., March 18, 7:30 p.m.
38 Special

Sat., March 19, 1 p.m.
Brad Paisley

Sat., March 19, 7:30 p.m.
Brad Paisley

Sun., March 20, 3 p.m.
Grupo Pesado

Tues., March 22, 7:30 p.m.
Clay Walker

Wed., March 23, 7:30 p.m.
Nelly

Thur., March 24, 7:30 p.m.
Kevin Fowler

Fri., March 25, 7:30 p.m.
Terri Clark

Sat., March 26, 7:30 p.m.
Rodeo Finals and
Joe Nichols

MARCH 12-26 2005

H·E·B   Ford   SOUTHWEST   Budweiser

Tickets available at HEB stores, on-line at www.RodeoAustin.com, or by phone at (512) 477-6060.

Star of Texas Fair and Rodeo ★ Travis County Expo Center

Promoting Youth Education – Preserving Western Heritage

Hadley Barrett has presided over the evolving show since the 1990s. He was joined in 2004 by PRCA Rodeo Clown Ash "Crash" Cooper, who helps keep the audience laughing and engaged between events. Wayne Brooks, 2005 and 2010 PRCA Announcer of the Year, teamed up with Barrett on the announcers' stand in 2005.

The charity added a Finals as part of the 13 nightly performances in 2002, which has helped build excitement over the multiday run and ensured that fans see the overall top performers. That audience extends worldwide via television broadcast as the organization negotiated the rights to televise its Xtreme Bull Riding competition on ESPN2 and the Pro-Rodeo Finals on the Outdoor Life Network in 2003. The networks agreed to broadcast on one condition—the Star of Texas Fair and Rodeo would have to rebrand the event to market it under a shorter name. "We chose the name Rodeo Austin. It was big hit and quickly has become synonymous with the entire 16-day fair and rodeo," Lamb said.

The performances have since been televised by Fox Sports and InCountry TV. In 2011, the Pursuit Channel broadcast the Rodeo Austin Finals to 38 million homes. In 2008, Rodeo Austin was the first in the world to be available as a pay-per-view webcast, with viewers as far away as China logging in to watch. Beginning in

Clinton Harlow, from Llano, and his border collie and cowboy monkey act entertained rodeo crowds during the 1970s. (Courtesy Carolyn and Alford Hill)

Kids aged five to seven try to hang on for a six-second ride during the Mutton Bustin' event held nightly during the ProRodeo. (Courtesy Star of Texas Fair and Rodeo)

Tommy Lucia, Whiplash the Cowboy Monkey, and dog Ben perform on the fairgrounds in 2010. (Courtesy Star of Texas Fair and Rodeo)

2009, the webcast was offered free to the U.S. military worldwide.

The organization took an unusual marketing step in 2006 by becoming the first ProRodeo to sponsor a rodeo team. Professional rodeo saddle bronc rider Chet Johnson and World Champion Bullfighter Lance Brittan were contracted as Team Rodeo Austin in 2006 and today serve as ambassadors for Rodeo Austin as they travel the rodeo circuit.

Rodeo Austin in 2011 was ranked seventeenth out of 600 PRCA rodeos nationwide and fifth among indoor regular-season rodeos in terms of the purse offered to winners, which was $412,458 that year. Longtime Rodeo Committee member Shaun Tuggle, who served as show president in 2008, said staying in the top PRCA tier is important to attract sponsorships and allows the charity to raise more money that can be funneled into its scholarships. "We've positioned ourselves dollar-wise to stay in the circuit to generate the enthusiasm and to get the top contestants here," Tuggle said.

Contestants also know they can count on good-quality rodeo stock to help them shine during competitions, Tuggle noted. The organization hired Bennie and Rhett Beutler of Elk City, Oklahoma, as stock contractors in 2005. The Beutlers bring more than 1,000 head of livestock to perform at Rodeo Austin each year and pasture them about 15 miles away from the Expo Center on veterinarian Charles Graham's ranch. "We bring in just enough stock each night to hold the performance," Lamb said. "They compete for eight seconds, then head back to green pastures and cool water." Professional saddle bronc rider Bonner Cooper said he can always expect a good "string of horses" whenever he competes at Rodeo Austin. "When the animals perform well, we perform well, too," he said.

Rodeo fans watch close-ups of barrel racers pulling tight turns and instant replays of bull riders' spills on four high-definition video screens hung high above the arena. Even though the venue is much larger than the rodeo's original one, the City Coliseum, ticket holders can still easily see the action and get caught up in the excitement on the arena floor. Those with front-row seats now sit six feet above the arena floor, not at bull's-eye level with their knees pressed up against a chain-link fence as fans were in the Coliseum. But they still have a chance of getting dirt kicked in their faces.

Cooper said he's seen Rodeo Austin grow considerably just in the last nine years he has been competing but that it still has an intimate feel. "It's becoming one of the better rodeos in Texas," Cooper said. "But it's a hometown feel at a big rodeo. It's definitely a neat experience."

All Around Champion Cowboys named by Rodeo Austin once received a set of spurs. (Courtesy Star of Texas Fair and Rodeo)

Team Rodeo Austin member Chet Johnson competes in the saddle bronc competition at Rodeo Austin in 2009. (Courtesy Star of Texas Fair and Rodeo)

As Team Rodeo Austin, world champion bullfighter Lance Brittan and professional rodeo saddle bronc rider Chet Johnson serve as ambassadors for the organization as they travel the rodeo circuit. (Courtesy Bucky Lamb)

In 2000 the Austin–Travis County Livestock Show and Rodeo implemented its plan to expand beyond its origins as a Travis County 4-H and FFA youth livestock show to stage an eight-county regional youth contest. But that was just the beginning—its ultimate aim was to encompass the state.

The charity needed a new identity to match these aspirations, and after its 2000 events were held, the organization rebranded itself the *Star of Texas Fair and Rodeo*. "Star" refers to the lone star used to mark Austin as the state capital on Texas maps. The group also hired a new general manager. Bucky Lamb, a Texas A&M University graduate who had been livestock manager of the San Antonio Stock Show & Rodeo for six years, came on board in April of that year. Lamb, who now holds the title chief

executive officer, said that during his first board of directors' meeting he challenged the group by saying, "Let's dream big and make it happen!" One of his first five actions was drafting a new mission statement: "Promoting Youth Education—Preserving Western Heritage."

Statewide Expansion, New Competitions

The 2000 Travis County show for 4-H and FFA youth was held in January at the Travis County Expo Center—earlier than usual. The first regional show, the ProRodeo, and the fairgrounds attractions were scheduled in March. The Travis County event became a ribbon show, rather than a terminal one, which allowed participants to bring their animals home afterward in case they wanted to enter them again in the regional show a couple of months later. From

2000 to 2005, the organization continued to host the Travis County youth show in addition to developing its new, regional show. In 2006, the Travis County Youth Show, a newly formed nonprofit, took over the county show from the Star of Texas Fair and Rodeo and runs it to this day.

Within eight years, the Star of Texas Fair and Rodeo methodically expanded its regional show to include entries from the entire state. The eight-county event held in 2000 expanded to 22 counties in 2001, grew to 45 counties in 2002 and 2003, then encompassed 120 counties in 2004 and 2005, and expanded to 190 counties in 2006. Tommy Dodd, president in 2006, ramped up statewide expansion plans by

announcing the show would go statewide in 2007. That year, the group held its first statewide youth livestock show for market animals. (Show organizers had staged a "statewide junior breeders" show as early as the mid-1950s.) The youth fair, which had begun in 1980, was held in conjunction with the Travis

Youth lead their hogs around the arena in controlled chaos as judges sort the top contestants in 2008. (Courtesy Star of Texas Fair and Rodeo)

A young man and his goats (muzzled to keep them from eating everything in sight) await the junior market goat competition in 2008. (Courtesy Star of Texas Fair and Rodeo)

Youth parade their steers before a judge in the Travis County Exposition Center show barn in 2008. (Courtesy Star of Texas Fair and Rodeo)

A judge surveys steers, some of which are taller than their exhibitors, during the 2009 livestock show. (Courtesy Star of Texas Fair and Rodeo)

County Livestock Show starting in 2000, and when the county show moved under the wing of the Travis County Youth Show, the youth fair went with it. "It was strategically the best thing to do," said Diron Blackburn, president in 2005.

"I always missed the youth fair, so when the idea of having a Western art show came up, I said absolutely, let's make that happen," Blackburn recalled. Executive liaison Jeff Nash led the effort to found the youth Western art competition in 2005, said Blackburn. A great deal of support also came from committee chair Dusty Black, who worked hard to ensure the new event's success. Winners received prizes and sold their art during an auction that year. "The art community in Austin was really gung-ho about it," Blackburn said. "We learned that there were people outside our rodeo community that could positively impact the show. It

was a learning experience for both groups. It proved that we could engage to promote the kids we both cared about."

Over time, additional non-livestock competitions have been added. "We want to grow where our roots are, but we also want our growth to encompass other youth [who can't or don't want to show livestock]," said Fred Weber, president in 2012. So in 2011, the charity unveiled two new competitions: the eco art youth recycling contest and the rodeo awesome reporter youth video journalism contest.

On and off throughout its history, horse shows had been part of the organization's annual livestock events, but by 2000 horses were no longer on the program. Bringing them back was one of many changes Lamb sought. "We made a big effort to have equestrian events," he said. "The number-one thing a fairgoer wants to see is a horse, and we didn't have a horse show." In 2008, the American Quarter Horse Association Horse Show joined the program. In 2009, so did the Collegiate Stock Horse of Texas Show, the Ranch Sorting Horse Show, and the Gold Stirrup Horse Show, a competition for children and adults with special needs. In 2010, an open horse show was added, and the Texas Draft Horse and Mule Show joined the ticket in 2011.

Youth Livestock Auction Receipts Grow

In 2007, the youth livestock auction, during which both winning livestock and Western art were sold, brought $650,138 to participants. Shaun Tuggle, president in 2008, said that following that sale, his focus was on increasing auction receipts. The organization's staff put together details from previous auctions and from auctions held by other Texas-wide shows. The group's Auction Committee incorporated a more formal structure into its work, including for the first time setting goals to help them achieve expected lot prices during the auction.

Auction sales grew to $825,471 in 2008.

Carly Lucas-Melanson of Dripping Springs High School won reserve grand champion for her entry in the 2008 Western art contest. (Courtesy Star of Texas Fair and Rodeo)

"We went from sitting in the show barn waiting to see who was going to show up and hopefully buy something to proactively raising money before the show," Tuggle said. "We're the last show on the circuit. The others [before ours] are terminal shows. If we don't make it worthwhile for everybody to feed another animal to bring here, we'll die a slow death," Tuggle said.

Kerry Wiggins, 2007 president, and Whitley James, a member of Live Oak County 4-H, stand outside the Long Center for the Performing Arts with James's grand champion goat in 2008. (Courtesy Star of Texas Fair and Rodeo)

"It was imperative to have a big, rewarding auction to generate enthusiasm around the state to get people to come."

In 2008, for the first time in the show's history, the winning livestock were not presented inside a dirt-filled arena or an outdoor ring before potential bidders. The youth auction moved into the brand-new Long Center for the Performing Arts at 701 West Riverside Drive in downtown Austin. Tuggle said show organizers wanted to get more central Austin business leaders involved in the event, so they thought, "Why not bring it to them" by moving the youth auction downtown. "It changed from an animal auction in a dusty, open-air barn to a youth auction in a downtown professional facility," Tuggle said. "It was a huge step. A big part of it was the visibility it provided."

In 2009, the youth auction moved to the Bob Bullock Texas State History Museum, at Eighteenth Street and Congress Avenue, where it and the annual Star of Texas Fair and Rodeo scholarship awards ceremony are held to this day. "It's the classiest environment of any youth auction in Texas and way beyond," Lamb said. "Students have the opportunity to not only see Texas history as they tour the museum that day but to be part of Texas history when they sell their prize-winning projects."

Since the auction takes place in the main lobby of the Bullock museum, visitors dropping by that day can witness the exciting action and get an up-close look at the grand champion steers, goats, lambs, and other livestock, which are presented in hay-lined pens outside the museum's entrance. Winning animals are no longer paraded before buyers. The students appear onstage beside photos of their winning entries as the auctioneers and "ring men" corral the frenetic bidding.

"Because we're in Central Texas with its high-tech environment, we've embraced video and show animal photos instead of the livestock," Lamb said. "We showcase the kid. It's about blue-ribbon kids, more than blue-ribbon animals." In 2009, the charity was the first organization of its kind to offer free Internet webcasting during the youth auction to expand its audience. "We weren't the first to use it to sell livestock. That was being done on ranches," said Johnny Philipello, Star of Texas Fair and Rodeo senior manager. "We just adopted an existing technology and applied it to the fair and livestock show industry. Now an uncle who lives in Washington and a grandma who lives in Omaha can bid on kids' projects. It's revolutionized our industry."

Despite the effect of the global recession of the late 2000s on the Austin and Texas economies, youth auction sales have remained strong, with $805,854.88 in receipts earned by students for their winning animals during 2011. Weber said he hopes the organization can garner enough support for the auction to hit $1 million in sales in 2012.

Haley Patke, a member of Bowie-Austin FFA, listens as buyers bid on her market roaster during the 2009 youth livestock auction at the Bob Bullock Texas State History Museum. (Courtesy Star of Texas Fair and Rodeo)

Austin Exemplified—High-Tech, Going Green, and 100-Plus Bands

The youth auction isn't the only area in which the organization has leveraged multimedia and high technology to make it easier for people to

From left to right, Miss Rodeo Austin Katie Crews, Cuatro Schauer, Doug Maund, and Miss Rodeo Austin Princess Stephanie Revels pose with Schauer's 2011 grand champion steer at the Bob Bullock Texas State History Museum after Maund placed the $60,000 winning bid for the steer at the youth auction. (Courtesy Star of Texas Fair and Rodeo)

learn about and support the Star of Texas Fair and Rodeo and to enjoy its events. Lamb said the charity's dynamic staff has been leading the way to embrace these tools. In 2003, Lamb negotiated the rights to nationally televise the ProRodeo Finals on ESPN2. The 2011 Finals were broadcast by the Pursuit Channel.

Then in 2004, the charity expanded its Web site. Today the site collects $1 million annually in online ticket sales. "In 2007, the Star of Texas Fair and Rodeo became the first to offer free Internet webcasting of the junior and open livestock shows," Philipello said. "The first webcam we put up in the show barn rafters cost $20 and didn't have sound. Today we have a webcasting budget of $15,000 a year, but tens of thousands of people are logging on to watch."

In 2010, the show became the first of its kind to offer an iPhone app as a guide to its annual festivities. Users download the application for free onto their iPhones and can use it to quickly scan information about the multitude of events offered each day during the 16-day production and even build their own custom schedule. The app's mapping feature helps users navigate the attraction-packed grounds when they visit.

Show leaders attribute much of the Star of Texas Fair and Rodeo's accomplishments since 2000 to inspiration the organization has drawn from the entrepreneurial, innovative spirit of its hometown. "We'll continue to push that envelope by virtue of being in Austin and around that Austin mentality," said Blackburn. In keeping with the Austin community's penchant for environmental conservation, the organization has since 2005 participated in Austin Energy's GreenChoice Program. The charity's corporate offices are powered with clean energy from renewable sources through the program. It also annually recycles 60 tons of plastic, paper, aluminum, wood shavings, and animal waste collected from the fairgounds.

In addition to its identity as a high-tech and green community, Austin likes to call itself the "live music capital of the world." No month better embodies that claim than does March, when the city is awash in live music performed by hundreds of bands drawn to town for the South by Southwest Music and Media Conference. The festival often overlaps with the Star of Texas Fair and Rodeo's two-plus weeks of events, which also include performances by more than 100 bands on the fairgrounds. National stars headline concerts after the ProRodeo. Patrons dance to live music at the 100X Club (which began in the early 1980s as the Stir*Up Club) or the

Bullet Proof party on the fairgrounds, each of which stays open until 2:00 A.M. Families can take in a free concert day or night as they chow down on corn dogs, pizza, and lemonade at the fairgrounds' Rockin' A outdoor stage.

Fun, Thrills, Laughs, and Learning

Since 2000, fairground offerings have continued to evolve to ensure visitors get a healthy dose of fun, thrills, laughs, and learning, with plenty of opportunities to nibble on a funnel cake while shopping for leather belts or jewelry. Many fairground attendees never make it

The Chow Town area of the fairgrounds provides a place to eat and relax outside the Luedecke Arena. (Courtesy Star of Texas Fair and Rodeo)

The petting zoo inside Kidstown on the fairgrounds gives children a chance to cuddle with, and learn about, farm animals. (Courtesy Star of Texas Fair and Rodeo)

Jersey cow Elsie and calf Beau, the milk company's mascots, are on hand, and for many kids it's the first time they have seen and touched a real, live cow. "I get asked [about Beau], 'Is that a reindeer?'" said Borden's Larry Campbell. "More and more kids are not around livestock."

A wander through the show barn on any given day during the annual event will reveal hundreds of lambs, steers, rabbits, miniature Herefords, and other livestock breeds being groomed and prepped by cowboy-booted 4-H or FFA kids or by adults competing in one of the open livestock shows gearing up for their time in the judging ring.

Attractions also include the largest carnival visiting Austin, run by Crabtree Amusements since 2001; a Buffalo Soldiers live historical exhibit; Texas Longhorn cattle; and the ever-popular pig races, which routinely elicit squeals of laughter from audience members, no matter their age. "It's a way to showcase Western heritage, Western values, and the Western way of life and to expose young people to what that's all about," Lamb said. "When you watch the racing pigs you're having a good time but you're learning."

The Star of Texas Fair and Rodeo mascots, Rusty Rodeo and Betsy Belle, traverse the fairgrounds greeting thousands. In 2011, 7,569 children visited the fairgrounds as part of the Star of Texas Fair and Rodeo's school tours program, and total fairground attendance topped 300,000. In 2011, parking cost $10; the fee to enter the fairgrounds was $7 for adults, $4 for kids. A combined rodeo-and-concert

inside the Luedecke Arena for the bull riding and barrel racing. "I think there is something for everyone. Not everyone wants to see a rodeo or a concert," Philipello said. "Maybe some people want to introduce their kids to where milk comes from."

Visitors to the Kidstown tent can hang out with deer, goats, and llamas in the petting zoo or watch a cow-milking demonstration. Borden's

Carnival rides provide thrills for all ages on the fairgrounds, including these junior pilots in 2009. (Courtesy Star of Texas Fair and Rodeo)

ticket ranged from $20 to $25 for a reserved seat in the stands and $37 for box seats to $175 for an Xtreme Seat (above the bucking chutes during the rodeo and on the arena floor for the concert).

Professional Staff and Economic Impact

The charity has had a 20-year collaboration with the University of Texas at Austin (UT) to manage its ticket sales. "David Hess serves as Texas Box Office manager for the University of Texas; however, in March Hess dons his cowboy hat and assumes the title of Star of Texas Fair

and Rodeo chief of ticketing," said Jennie Richmond, Star of Texas Fair and Rodeo marketing manager. "No one knows ticketing better than this guy. He's basically sold every ticket that's been sold here for twenty years. The University of Texas has contributed to our scholarship mission by offering us low Texas Box Office fees."

The Star of Texas Fair and Rodeo today depends upon help from more than 700 such contractors, seasonal staff, and college interns in addition to some 1,500 dedicated volunteers serving on 29 committees that run everything from the organization's gala—its biggest

Star of Texas Fair and Rodeo mascot Rusty Rodeo makes visitors welcome on the fairgrounds. (Courtesy Star of Texas Fair and Rodeo)

fund-raiser—to the barbecue cook-off, the calf scramble, and the cowboy breakfast.

The organization's full-time staff has grown since 2000 to total 14 in 2011. "The staff work more than 100 hours a week during the fair and rodeo. They don't take a day off for over a month," Lamb said. "Every Team Rodeo Austin member is truly dedicated to our mission. Senior managers Katy Blankinship and Johnny Philipello and marketing manager Jennie Richmond have carried a whole lot of water for this organization."

A junior baker prepares biscuits at a chuck wagon on the fairgrounds of the Travis County Exposition Center. (Courtesy Star of Texas Fair and Rodeo)

As its programs and activities have grown, so has the organization's economic impact upon the Austin area. After learning that City of Austin leaders did not fully recognize and appreciate its contribution to the community, the organization commissioned an economic impact study from UT's College of Communications, Department of Advertising, in 2004. The research showed that the charity generated $45 million annually for Central Texas. A more detailed study the organization commissioned in 2008 from the firm Texas Perspectives (now called TXP, Inc.) found that the Star of Texas Fair and Rodeo generated more than $54 million annually for the region. (A study conducted as early as 1986 estimated that the livestock show and rodeo's economic impact on Central Texas totaled $26 million, according to *Austin American-Statesman* columnist Paul Bailey, who wrote about it in 1988.) "We were thinking we really wanted people to know who we are and what kind of impact we have," Blackburn said. "When they said we had a multi-million dollar impact, the city listened. We met several times with the mayor." In 2011, the impact had grown to exceed $68 million annually.

The Star of Texas Fair and Rodeo's marketing efforts have gone into high gear since 2000. In 2003, the Rodeo Austin brand was created with its logo of an upside-down "hookin' A" fashioned to resemble steer horns. The image is now found on everything from baseball caps, T-shirts, and lapel pins to folding chairs and foam hands.

In 2004, the charity moved its annual gala, its top fund-raising event, out of the Luedecke

(Courtesy Star of Texas Fair and Rodeo)

Arena and into the recently constructed Palmer Events Center in central Austin. Richard Hill, president in 2004, is credited as the visionary behind this decision. Staging this black-tie and boots event in Palmer greatly elevated its status within the community. The gala is now one of the most important "see-and-be-seen" fetes on Austin's social calendar. Annually, more than 2,000 pack the hall to bid on over 100 items in a silent auction, dine on a four-course meal, and listen to top entertainers such as Brooks & Dunn and Martina McBride.

Another turning point for the charity came in 2007 when it released the marketing firm it had been contracting with and brought all creative, promotional efforts in-house. "That was a huge step," Tuggle said. "You look at the creative awards, advertising awards, and innovation awards hanging around this place. Our marketing staff, led by Jennie Richmond, has gotten us away from the stigma of the old bunch of redneck rodeo guys out here playin' in the dirt for thirty days. People now realize we're a professional organization."

The Star of Texas Fair and Rodeo's marketing staff launched an annual campaign to promote the organization's March events, which have now collectively become known as Rodeo Austin, using tag lines such as "Live Action, Live Music and Live Stock" and "Where Weird Meets Western." A biannual, full-color newsletter, *Behind the Chutes*, highlights the organization's latest accomplishments and upcoming events. Staff also make public presentations and get the word out about the charity's activities through social media, including social networking sites Facebook and Twitter. However, the wider public awareness and increased attendance in aging facilities has left the group once again facing what has become a recurring challenge throughout its history.

Growing Pains

In 1997, the Star of Texas Fair and Rodeo purchased 45 acres at 9100 Decker Lake Road. This prime location adjacent to the Expo Center's 128 acres has served as parking for growing crowds. The next year, the group constructed a 9,500-square-foot building to serve as a logistical command center during its annual events, and in 2006, the charity constructed a permanent office. Stan Voelker's (president in 1999) company bid to construct the building at an economical price so more funds could be given to students in the form of

Thousands of supporters pack Palmer Events Center in 2008 for the annual Rodeo Austin Gala, which featured country-music singer Josh Turner. (Courtesy Star of Texas Fair and Rodeo)

CHAPTER 6

scholarships. Staff moved into the new building, named the Dr. Charles W. Graham Western Heritage Center, in 2006.

These improvements have made working conditions better, but the Expo Center facilities and available event parking are being pushed to their limits. With the addition of new livestock and horse show competitions since 2000, the volume of people and animals overtaxes the 210,000-square-foot show barn's pens as well as its electrical and water systems. The Luedecke Arena often sees the rodeo sell out with standing-room-only crowds at the most popular concerts, and 7,000 parking spaces are routinely maxed out. Several show leaders said they believe the organization is being constrained by the capacity and the quality of the facilities at the Expo Center. The Star of Texas Fair and Rodeo has formed a Long-Range Planning Committee and conducted facility feasibility studies and demographic research to help it determine how best to deal with this issue.

Throughout its history, the organization has more than once outgrown its home and had to find or build a new one. Today the group has a sense of déjà vu. "We've created our own challenges because we've been so successful," Lamb said. "We're the fastest-growing livestock show and ProRodeo in the nation. But currently, we're like a racehorse with someone pulling back on the reins. We can't truly show what we're capable of because the facilities are stopping us. If we're able to build new facilities, we'll be able to achieve greater things."

A Challenging, Bright Future

Today more than a dozen past presidents remain dedicated to the show's mission and serve either on its 82-member board, its Executive Committee, or a volunteer committee. Some directors said the key to a successful future means drawing upon this seasoned experience—which stretches back three decades—while recruiting new participants.

"I think we'll continue to grow the show in a variety of ways, but it's really going to depend on us as a board. We need to continue to educate and engage our existing board members and get new board members who are community leaders and who believe in our mission," Tuggle said. "The other important component is keeping our experienced leaders engaged. We really have to rely on their knowledge and leadership and what they bring to the table with their history. We need their contacts and guidance, and we need them to help develop the next generation of leaders." Leaders hope the organization will make continued strides in recruiting volunteers and leaders from areas of the community that haven't been fully tapped. "I think we have a solid future," said Haskell Griffin, president in 1996. "A lot depends on how we can transition into either having a larger volunteer base that touches different parts of the entire city or having a director base that touches key parts of the community where the money is."

The show is trying to expand community participation at all levels. Directors have typically been men, although the Star of Texas Fair

Veterinarian Charles Graham (center right with scissors) cuts the rope at the 2006 opening of the Star of Texas Fair and Rodeo's newly constructed offices, adjacent to the Travis County Exposition Center. Graham's support helped make the building possible. Standing with him are (left to right) Star of Texas Fair and Rodeo Chief Executive Officer Bucky Lamb, rodeo stock contractor Bennie Beutler, rodeo announcer Wayne Brooks, Jay Gray, Star of Texas Fair and Rodeo 2006 President Tommy Dodd, Star of Texas Fair and Rodeo Director Tyler Graham, rodeo announcer Hadley Barrett, Star of Texas Fair and Rodeo 2007 President Kerry Wiggins, and Star of Texas Fair and Rodeo 2010 President Bryan Teich. (Courtesy Star of Texas Fair and Rodeo)

and Rodeo has 12 women serving on its board and women routinely chair and participate in volunteer committees. In 2011, women made up 61 percent of the 29 committee chairs and 49 percent of the more than 1,500 volunteers. The charity has had one minority president so far and is working to develop new leaders who represent Texas' diversity. "We welcome a more diverse board of directors. We welcome diverse cultures. We welcome people from all races and sexes and creeds to be part of this effort to advance children's dreams," Lamb said. "Our scholarships are open to students from all walks of life, and we believe our volunteer force as well as our staff should reflect this."

Changes in the livestock show and fair industry and in the sport of ProRodeo have to be anticipated and adapted to while remaining focused on the Star of Texas Fair and Rodeo's mission, said Mike Eledge, a board member who served as president in 1986. "I think we have to look at our mission and understand that we're still working for young people and that's what we're here about," Eledge said. "Some of the other big shows are contemplating very major changes. We have a bright future, but if you think it's going to be the same as what you were doing, you are wrong. You better get ready to lead, follow, or get the hell out of the way."

Long-range planning will continue to play a crucial role to help the charity cope with these and other changes while focusing on its mission. "We've been working hard on our long-range planning and want to highlight all that we are doing and how much we have already done for youth," Weber said. "I believe that our planning combined with increased community awareness of our mission will catapult us forward."

What started out as a tiny event sponsored by the Austin Chamber of Commerce to educate 4-H and FFA youth and adults about how best to raise calves for the marketplace is today one of Austin's largest charities assisting thousands of students annually. The organization awarded more than $5 million in college scholarships as of 2011. Over the past 30 years, through its scholarships and other programs, Texas youth have received more than $30 million. Lamb said the charity's legacy lies within its scholarship recipients. "We're here to make their dreams become reality. Only when their contributions to humanity and the planet are realized will we truly know the impact of the Star of Texas Fair and Rodeo."

SCHOLARSHIPS AT THE HEART OF CHARITY'S MISSION

Although the Star of Texas Fair and Rodeo's ProRodeo, livestock show, and bustling fairgrounds each March are what the organization is primarily known for, its scholarship program is at the heart of the charity's mission. Since 1981, the organization has awarded over $5 million in scholarships to 2,140 recipients—beneficiaries of the group's year-round fundraising efforts.

Each year, the organization awards dozens of scholarships to students from across Texas planning to attend colleges and universities in the state. The awards, which average $9,400 and range in value from $2,500 to $16,000, help outstanding students pursue degrees in everything from biomedical engineering, accounting, and environmental design to sociology, sports journalism, and animal science. "In 2011 alone, we presented 46 students with scholarships totaling $442,000," said Calley Callahan Asklund, Scholarship Committee chair. "These young people are from all walks of life and may pursue any degree plan. Eighty-three percent came from urban or suburban backgrounds, and 49 percent live in households with annual incomes totaling $50,000 or less."

The organization partners with the University of Texas, Texas A&M University, Texas State University, Texas Tech University, Austin Community College, St. Edward's University, Concordia University Texas, Huston-Tillotson University, West Texas A&M University, and Sam Houston State University, as well as the Texas 4-H Foundation and the Texas FFA Foun-

dation. These institutions select the winners. During the screening process, each applicant's degree of financial need, grade-point average, class rank, and SAT and ACT scores, as well as their extracurricular activities, are considered.

Although the charity officially launched its scholarship program in 1981, when nine high school graduates received $500 each to help them with their first year of college, it gave a few scholarships to students at least as early as 1972. That year two girls chosen from area FFA and 4-H clubs as the show's princesses received "a certificate denoting a $200 college scholarship to the college or university of their choice." The show also provided princesses with Western outfits—including suits, boots, and hats—and hosted them throughout the show. Today the winners of Miss Rodeo Austin and Miss Rodeo Austin Princess are awarded college scholarships of $16,000 and $10,000, respectively.

When the scholarship program began in 1981, those first students were required to have participated in the livestock show, but that is not the case today. A few winners have experience raising and showing livestock or are budding rodeo athletes, but most have no connection to agriculture. Many have never even attended a livestock show or a rodeo.

In 2006, Bonner Cooper of Lubbock was the first to receive a Star of Texas Fair and Rodeo scholarship to attend graduate school. Cooper used the $5,000 award to obtain a master's degree in marketing at Texas A&M University. "Pursing my master's was always my goal,"

Cooper said. "Receiving the scholarship alleviated a lot of the burden I would have had to endure. It really helped me achieve my goals both in and out of the classroom." Following graduation, Cooper has worked in sports marketing and as a saddle bronc rider on the professional rodeo circuit.

Amber Abadie of Cedar Park said she had always dreamed of becoming a teacher, and the $5,000 scholarship she received in 2010 is helping her pursue that dream. She is studying elementary education at Austin Community College. "The scholarship gives me and my family financial stability," Abadie said. "It gives me a way to pay for college without taking out loans."

The Star of Texas Fair and Rodeo is one of Central Texas' largest nonprofit collegiate scholarship providers. As the costs of higher education continue to mount, the organization has used a variety of fund-raising methods to increase scholarship giving. Some scholarships are directly funded through sponsorships. Several organizations and businesses have funded individual Star of Texas Fair and Rodeo scholarships over the years. One of the first sponsors in the early 1980s was Mr. Gatti's Pizza. Most recently, Silicon Laboratories has underwritten scholarships to individuals pursuing degrees in science or math. Scholarship coffers also benefit during the annual youth livestock auctions. Caps set on sales prices ensure that when a winning bid on an animal is higher than the cap, the extra cash is swept into the scholarship fund.

In addition, several year-round efforts managed by volunteer committees raise money,

sometimes by combining hard work with a bit of merrymaking. The Star of Texas Fair and Rodeo's annual gala, barbecue cook-off, golf tournament, sporting clay shoot, and other annual events offer participants a good time for a good cause. Likewise, the 100X Club, open on the fairgrounds during the rodeo, and the Bullet Proof party, a two-night blowout held during the rodeo's last weekend, offer patrons food, drinks, live music, and a chance to mingle with rodeo cowboys. Club members, party sponsors, and their guests have a good time while knowing the money collected through fees and their donations help build the scholarship fund.

The Austin Tequila Society from the late 1980s to 2000 defined the fund-raise-while-you-party concept. "In all, the group raised about $250,000 for the organization's scholarships and another $250,000 to establish an endowment for the program," said Ted Nagel, president in 1981 and Scholarship Committee chairman during part of the 1980s and 1990s. The endowment set up by the Austin Tequila Society, now known as the Austin Endowment Society, is today the largest of the 32 endowments that supporters have established to provide long-term support for the program. In all, these totaled $914,668 in 2011. Nagel said the idea to establish a scholarship program came from Robert Sneed, president in 1980. Before then, show leaders hoped kids who sold winning livestock at the auction would put the funds away for college, but there was no requirement to do so.

There is no better place for Star of Texas Fair and Rodeo supporters to witness the fruits of their labors than to attend the annual scholarship awards ceremony held at the Bob

Bullock Texas State History Museum, said Diron Blackburn, president in 2005. "The story that sticks out in my mind is the scholarship banquet we had the year I was president. A young man from Cedar Park was going to the fire academy through Austin Community College," Blackburn said. "He said 'My family could not afford for me to go to school without this. I want to be a fireman, and I want to help people. Maybe one day when one of you is in need, I can save you and I'll pay you back.' It was powerful. That was his dream, and we were able to help push that forward. That makes it all worth it," Blackburn said. "I'm sure there are thousands of stories just like that out there."

April 4, 1985

acbils
500 club

Dear Mr. Sneed,
  I would like to thank you for sponsoring my scholarship. It makes me happy, to know that y'all are out there supporting us and our livestock. But it makes me more happy to realize y'all are still supporting us as we graduate and go on to college.
  Thank you again for your support, and I hope you will continue to support the Austin Harris County Livestock Show.
                    Sincerely,
                    Lisa Pfluger

Longtime show supporter Robert Sneed, thanked here, is one of the individuals credited with founding the organization's scholarship program in 1980. (Courtesy Star of Texas Fair and Rodeo)

96

Recipients awarded Star of Texas Fair and Rodeo college scholarships in 2010 gather in front of the Bob Bullock Texas State History Museum. (Courtesy Star of Texas Fair and Rodeo)

DIRECTORS EMERITI

The highest honor a director of the Star of Texas Fair and Rodeo can attain is to be granted the lifelong position of Director Emeritus. As stated in the bylaws of the organization, a Director Emeritus "in the opinion of the Board, has served with distinction and provided services and/or resources over and above the ordinary given service of a Director." The following individuals have achieved Director Emeritus status:

Robert Sneed
Mike Levi
Jimmy Callahan
Verlin Callahan
Jay Evans
Bill Knolle
Ted Nagel

SHOW LEADERS

1940   George C. Quinn, committee chairman

1941   George C. Quinn, committee chairman

1942   Ernest Best, committee chairman

1943   Joe C. Carrington, committee chairman

1944   Joe C. Carrington, committee chairman

1945   Joe C. Carrington, committee chairman
       Elwood Nelson, junior president

1946   Joe C. Carrington, committee chairman

1947   Johnny L. Moulden, committee chairman

1948   Johnny L. Moulden, committee chairman

1949   Johnny L. Moulden, committee chairman

1950   Claude Voyles, president, Capital Area Farm and Ranch Club

1951   August Kaufman, president, Capital Area Farm and Ranch Club

1952   C. J. Schmid, president, Capital Area Farm and Ranch Club

1953   C. J. Schmid, president, Capital Area Farm and Ranch Club

1954   Charles D. Nash, president, Capital Area Farm and Ranch Club

1955   Victor H. Randolph, president, Capital Area Farm and Ranch Club

1956   Victor H. Randolph, president, Capital Area Farm and Ranch Club

1957   George Riggin, chairman
       Lynn Griffin, Austin Chamber of Commerce agricultural manager

1958   George Riggin, chairman
       Lynn Griffin, Austin Chamber of Commerce agricultural manager

1959   Charles Nash, chairman
       Lynn Griffin, Austin Chamber of Commerce agricultural manager

1960   Alvin G. East, chairman
       Lynn Griffin, Austin Chamber of Commerce agricultural manager

1961   David Gault, chairman
       Lynn Griffin, Austin Chamber of Commerce agricultural manager

1962   Dunning Bright, chairman
       Lynn Griffin, Austin Chamber of Commerce agricultural manager

1963   L. D. Steffens, chairman
       Lynn Griffin, Austin Chamber of Commerce agricultural manager

1964   Lynn Storm, chairman
       Lynn Griffin, Austin Chamber of Commerce agricultural manager

1965   Jim Boswell, chairman
       Lynn Griffin, Austin Chamber of Commerce agricultural manager

1966   Jim A. Morriss, chairman
       Lynn Griffin, Austin Chamber of Commerce agricultural manager

1967   L. E. (Bubba) Duncan, chairman
       Lynn Griffin, Austin Chamber of Commerce agricultural manager

1968   Norman Bonnett, chairman
       Lynn Griffin, Austin Chamber of Commerce agricultural manager

1969   George O. Slaughter, president
       Lynn Griffin, Austin Chamber of Commerce agricultural manager

1970   George O. Slaughter, president
       Lynn Griffin, Austin Chamber of Commerce agricultural manager

1971   C. D. (Doc) McEver, president
       Lynn Griffin, Austin Chamber of Commerce agricultural manager

1972   Verlin Callahan, president
       Lynn Griffin, Austin Chamber of Commerce agricultural manager

1973   Verlin Callahan, president
Lynn Griffin, Austin Chamber of Commerce
agricultural manager
1974   Doug Nichols, president
Lynn Griffin, Austin Chamber of Commerce
agricultural manager
1975   Johnny Gustafson, president
Art Keller, Austin Chamber of Commerce
staff
1976   Neal Johnson, president
Art Keller, Austin Chamber of Commerce
staff
1977   Bill Hamilton, president
Art Keller, Austin Chamber of Commerce
staff
1978   Bill Hamilton, president
Art Keller, Austin Chamber of Commerce
staff
1979   Jay Evans, president
Art Keller, Austin Chamber of Commerce
staff
1980   Robert Sneed, president
Kenneth Hees, executive director
1981   Ted Nagel, president
Kenneth Hees, executive director
1982   John Baker, president
Kenneth Hees, executive director
1983   Jimmy Callahan, president
Kenneth Hees, executive director
1984   Bill Knolle, president
Kenneth Hees, executive director
1985   Jay Evans, president
Kenneth Hees, executive director
1986   Mike Eledge, president
Dick Engle, executive director
1987   John Weisman, president
Dick Engle, executive director
1988   Thomas Carlson, president
Dick Engle, executive director
1989   Robert Lanford, president
Dick Engle, executive director
1990   Mike Levi, president
Linda Raven, executive director

1991   Bob Avant, president
Linda Raven, executive director
1992   Jimmy Evans, president
Linda Raven, executive director
1993   Terrell Hamann, president
Linda Raven, executive director
1994   Jeff Nash, president
Linda Raven, executive director
1995   Curtis Calhoun, president
Linda Raven, executive director
1996   Haskell Griffin, president
Linda Raven, executive director
1997   Jim Achilles, president
Linda Raven, executive director
1998   Hil Stroup, president
Linda Raven, executive director
1999   Stan Voelker, president
Linda Raven, executive director
2000   Donnie Williams, president
Linda Raven, executive director
2001   Keith Crawford, president
Bucky Lamb, general manager
2002   Don Holcomb, president
Bucky Lamb, general manager
2003   Steve Skinner, president
Bucky Lamb, general manager
2004   Richard Hill, president
Bucky Lamb, general manager
2005   Diron Blackburn, president
Bucky Lamb, general manager
2006   Tommy Dodd, president
Bucky Lamb, general manager
2007   Kerry Wiggins, president
Bucky Lamb, general manager
2008   Shaun Tuggle, president
Bucky Lamb, general manager
2009   Gilbert Turrieta, president
Bucky Lamb, general manager
2010   Bryan Teich, president
Bucky Lamb, chief executive officer
2011   Travis Asklund, president
Bucky Lamb, chief executive officer
2012   Fred Weber, president
Bucky Lamb, chief executive officer

GRAND CHAMPION WINNERS AND BUYERS

This list includes the owners/exhibitors of the show's grand champion market steers, where they were from or what 4-H or FFA club they belonged to, the prices paid for the steers at auction, and who purchased them.

1940 Vernon Carson, Creedmoor, $207.63, Harry Akin of Night Hawk Restaurants

1941 Vernon Carson, Creedmoor, $425.25, Austin & Barrow

1942 Ted Lehman, Pilot Knob, $380.00, Harry Akin of Night Hawk Restaurants

1943 Ted Lehman, Pilot Knob, $0.57 per pound, The Chicken Shack

1944 Vincent Nelson, Elroy, $637.50, El Charro Cafe

1945 Joe Ed Johnson, Creedmoor, $1,258.75, El Charro 1

1946 Gordon Berggren, Lund, $671.25, Kash-Karry Stores

1947 Warren Smith, Dessau, $686.25, Kash-Karry Stores

1948 Lowell Berggren, Lund, $585.00, Kash-Karry Stores

1949 Ed Willingham, Austin, $840.00, Lem Scarbrough Foundation of Austin

1950 Kermit Hees, Pflugerville, $1,474.00, Harry Akin of Night Hawk Restaurants

1951 Ed Willingham, Austin, $1,920.00, Grand Prize Brewing Company

1952 Curtis Neidig, Elgin, $1,500.00, Piccadilly Cafeteria

1953 Roland Wieland, Pflugerville, $1,040.00, W. O. Stone of Food Mart Stores

1954 Larry Pfluger, Pflugerville, $1,720.00, W. W. Heath of Circle-Bar Ranch

1955 Robert Pfluger, Pflugerville, $1,000.00, Lone Star Brewery

1956 Wilbert Becker, Pflugerville, $1,457.00, Lone Star Brewery

1957 Howard Meiske, Pflugerville, $820.00, Alvin East of L. East Produce Company

1958 Howard Meiske, Pflugerville, $1,880.00, James D. Culp of Culp's Foodland Stores

1959 Wilbert Becker, Pflugerville, $1,484.00, James D. Culp of Culp's Foodland Stores

1960 Glenn Weiss, Pflugerville, $985.00, Rylander Food Stores

1961 Michael Smith, Austin, $652.57, A. L. Rice of Lone Star Brewery

1962 Bobby Gene Le Doux, Manchaca, $955.00, C. O. Maltsberger of the Roegelein Provision Company

1963 Bobby Gene Le Doux, Manchaca, $930.00, Capital Plaza Shopping Center

1964 Gordon Smith, Del Valle, $2,164.00, Harry Akin of Night Hawk Restaurants

1965 Gordon Smith, Del Valle, $1,709.00, Harry Akin of Night Hawk Restaurants

1966 Barbara Melber, Pflugerville, $2,808.00, Harry Akin of Night Hawk Restaurants

1967 Gordon Smith, Del Valle, $3,397.60, Jack Ray of The Barn Restaurant

1968 Margaret Hees, Pflugerville, $2,652.80, American National Bank

1969 Margaret Hees, Pflugerville, $2,677.50, American National Bank

1970 Margaret Hees, Pflugerville, $2,784.00, Jack Ray of The Barn Restaurant

1971   Mark Hodgson, Pflugerville, $3,114.00, Capital National Bank

1972   Lary Lawrence, Pflugerville, $3,682.00, City National Bank

1973   Lary Lawrence, Pflugerville, $4,495.40, Louis J. Luedecke

1974   Jamie Collins, Pflugerville, $5,310.00, Austin Clearing House Association

1975   Pam Samuelson, Manda 4-H, $5,525.00, Austin National Bank

1976   Eric Hodgson, Pflugerville, $7,720.00, Bob Gray

1977   Lary Lawrence, Pflugerville FFA, $9,234.00, Lowell Lebermann Jr. and Lincoln Mercury Ford

1978   Lary Lawrence, Pflugerville FFA, $9,582.30, Capital National Bank

1979   Don Lundgren, Manda 4-H, $11,930.00, Tim Dorsett of the 221 Pit Stop

1980   Amy Lindgren, Manda 4-H, $13,900.25, Tim Dorsett of the 221 Pit Stop

1981   Debbie Hees, Richland 4-H, $20,461.00, Tom Coffman of Coffman Cattle Company

1982   Amy Lindgren, Manda 4-H, $14,362.00, Preston Harvey Construction Co. and the Break Time Coffee Service

1983   Lorren Mott, Pflugerville FFA, $17,919.00, Jim Boyce of Boyce Iron Works

1984   Jon Bishop, Pflugerville 4-H, $21,000.00, Tim Dorsett of Dorsett Construction Co.

1985   Brenda Oertli, Pflugerville 4-H, $24,000.00, Earle Weekly Builders and Boyce Iron Works

1986   Antonio Galvan, Richland 4-H, $17,000.00, Air Conditioning Incorporated

1987   Joy Oertli, Der Kamper 4-H, $17,050.00, Joe McDaniel and Mrs. Albert Priem

1988   Jason Weiss, Richland 4-H, $7,000.00, Capital Feed and Milling and Callahan's General Store

1989   William Kaderka, Pflugerville FFA, $10,000.00, Tom Ford of Sirloin Stockade and Jerry Oertli of Sandy Creek Ranch

1990   Jason Weiss, Richland 4-H, $9,175.00, Sirloin Stockade and Paleface Ranch

1991   Jimmy Galvan, Richland 4-H, $11,000.00, Sirloin Stockade and Callahan's General Store

1992   Stephen Schleuter, Lanier FFA, $20,000.00, Beatrice McQueen

1993   Robin Oertli, Cele 4-H, $25,000.00, Jack Carmody of Ranger Excavating

1994   Katherine Wilke, Pflugerville FFA, $20,000.00, Beatrice McQueen

1995   Randall Hees, Richland 4-H, $27,500.00, McCarty Corporation

1996   Melanie Atwood, Pflugerville FFA, $30,000.00, Beatrice McQueen

1997   Greg Balderas, Cele 4-H, $50,000.00, Richard Wallrath of Champion Window

1998   Brandy Murchison, Pflugerville, $60,000.00, Richard Wallrath of Champion Window

1999   Brandy Murchison, Cele 4-H, $70,000.00, Richard Wallrath of Champion Window

2000   Lauren Schroeder, Williamson Co. 4-H, $100,000.00, Richard Wallrath of Champion Window

2001   Brittany Barton, Jarrell, $102,000.00, Richard Wallrath of Champion Window

2002   Mary Perry, Gillespie Co 4-H, $107,000.00, McCarty Corporation

2003   Justin Kelly, Gonzales Co. 4-H, $75,000.00, Champion Ranch

2004   Tate McCarty, Parker Co. 4-H, $50,000.00, Steer Syndicate and Richard Hill

2005   Hayes Hill, Jones Co. 4-H, $60,000.00, McCarty Corporation

2006   Travis Turner, McLennan Co. 4-H, $75,000.00, H-E-B and Ford Motor Company

2007   Reagan Tucker, Williamson Co. 4-H, $34,150.00, Lammes Candies, William Gammon Insurance, Williamson County Buyers Group, Toyota, Rick Lange, H-E-B, Fred Weber, Callahan's General Store,

Berdoll Pecans, Austin Foam Plastics, BBQ Buyers Group

2008   Jamie Mitchell, Glen Rose FFA, $50,000.00, McCarty Corporation

2009   Hayden Tucker, Williamson Co. 4-H, $50,000.00, McCarty Corporation

2010   Kaycie Carter, Caney Creek FFA, $57,000.00, McCarty Corporation

2011   Cuatro Schauer, Bee County 4-H, $60,000.00, Doug Maund

ABOUT THE RESEARCH

The research for this book took about a year to complete. The libraries and archives I used included the Austin History Center, the Dolph Briscoe Center for American History at the University of Texas at Austin, the Texas State Library and Archives, the Travis County archives, and the archives of the Star of Texas Fair and Rodeo. I conducted more than 25 interviews with the organization's volunteer leaders, other volunteers, staff, and rodeo participants. I also spoke with livestock show and Western art show participants and their parents and scholarship winners and their parents.

Since 1988, many have thought that the first livestock show in the group's history was held in 1938. The evidence cited for this was a photograph of livestock show participant Raymond Hees, Molly O'Daniel (Governor W. Lee "Pappy" O'Daniel's daughter), and Hees's prize-winning steer standing together with the State Capitol dome in the background. This photo was thought to have originally appeared in a 1938 issue of an Austin daily newspaper. Several times, the Star of Texas Fair and Rodeo staff and I scoured the microfilm copies of the dailies looking for the photo from that time period but came up empty-handed. However, my research found two primary sources that date the founding of the show. The Chamber of Commerce annual reports for that period state that the chamber began planning its first Baby Beef Show in 1938 and held the first show in 1940. Additionally, the *Austin Statesman* reported on March 7, 1940, on what it called Austin's first Baby Beef Show.

Instead of including a detailed list of my sources, I have provided a more condensed, general collection of the documents I used organized by each chapter and featured topic within the book. I did not include sources for chapter 1 since this is an overview. Those facts and their sources are included throughout the book's other chapters. I used information gleaned from interviews in each chapter and particularly relied upon them in chapter 6.

Chapter 2

Sixteenth Census of the United States: 1940, Agriculture, vol. 1, part 5; annual reports, Austin Chamber of Commerce, 1930s, 1940s; *Morrison & Fourmy's Austin City Directory*, 1939, 1940; *General Facts and Statistical Review on Austin, Texas, 1940*, Austin Chamber of Commerce; unpublished manuscripts, correspondence, chamber meeting minutes, and other documents in the Walter E. Long collection, Austin History Center; vertical files, Livestock Show, Austin History Center; *Austin in Action* magazine, Austin Chamber of Commerce, 1953; articles, editorials, photographs, and Rueben's Half

Acre column in the *Austin American*, the *Austin Statesman*, and the *Austin American-Statesman* daily newspapers, 1938 through 1956.

Early Education Develops Local Livestock Market

Annual reports, Austin Chamber of Commerce, 1940, 1943; 1945 U.S. Government Agricultural Census; articles in the *Austin Statesman*, 1940.

Rodeo and Livestock Show Royalty

Austin magazine, Austin Chamber of Commerce, March 1969, March 1972; articles in the *Austin American-Statesman*, 1954, 1967, 1988.

Chapter 3

Annual reports, Austin Chamber of Commerce, 1950s, 1960s; *Austin in Action* magazine, Austin Chamber of Commerce, 1966; *Austin* magazine, Austin Chamber of Commerce, March issues in 1960s, 1970s; vertical files, Livestock Show, Austin History Center; documents from the Star of Texas Fair and Rodeo archives, including "A Brief Summary of the Highlights of the Austin Livestock Show: 1956–1976," and correspondence, programs, and show brochures; articles, editorials, photographs, and Farm Roundup column in the *Austin American*, the *Austin Statesman*, and the *Austin American-Statesman*, 1957 through 1979.

Supporters Key to Success

Annual reports, Austin Chamber of Commerce, 1940s; Travis County Commissioners meeting minutes, 1975, 1978; *Austin* magazine, Austin Chamber of Commerce, March 1984; Lynn Griffin correspondence, 1966, Star of Texas Fair and Rodeo archives; articles in the *Austin American*, the *Austin Statesman*, and the *Austin American-Statesman*, 1940s, 1950s.

Chapter 4

Documents from the Star of Texas Fair and Rodeo archives, including "President's Report: A.T.C.L.S–1980–81," "Austin–Travis County Livestock Show 1997 Fact Sheet," correspondence, newsletters, programs, and brochures; *Austin* magazine, Austin Chamber of Commerce, March 1982, March 1984; Travis County archives, 1966, 1988, 1989; Austin City Council minutes, March 14, 1985; articles in the *Austin American-Statesman*, 1980s.

Parades Brought Western Heritage to Capital City

Documents from the Star of Texas Fair and Rodeo archives, including "1980 Livestock Show Parade"; *Austin in Action* magazine, Austin Chamber of Commerce, 1955; articles from the *Austin American*, the *Austin Statesman*, and the *Austin American-Statesman*, 1950s, 1970s, 1980s, 2000.

Chapter 5

Sixteenth Census of the United States: 1940, Agriculture, vol. 1, part 5; 1992 U.S. Government Census of Agriculture–County Data, Travis County, Texas; *Morrison & Fourmy's Austin*

City Directory, 1942; documents from the Star of Texas Fair and Rodeo archives, including "Austin–Travis County Livestock Show 1997 Fact Sheet," "1990 Champions," newsletters, board meeting minutes; vertical files, Livestock Show, Austin History Center; articles in the *Austin American-Statesman*, 1990s, 2000.

ProRodeo Evolved from Calf
Scrambles in 1949

Austin magazine, Austin Chamber of Commerce, March 1969; vertical files, Rodeos, Austin History Center, including unpublished report by Paul Eby, "Austin Jr. Rodeo," May 23, 1952; articles from the *Austin American*, the *Austin Statesman*, and the *Austin American-Statesman*, 1940s, 1950s, 1980s, 1990s.

Chapter 6

Documents from the Star of Texas Fair and Rodeo archives, including programs, newsletters, and news releases; Star of Texas Fair and Rodeo Web site, www.rodeoaustin.com; articles in the *Austin American-Statesman*, 1988, 2000–2010.

Scholarships at the Heart
of Charity's Mission

Documents from the Star of Texas Fair and Rodeo archives, including 1981 letter listing first scholarship recipients; *Austin* magazine, Austin Chamber of Commerce, March 1972; Star of Texas Fair and Rodeo Web site, www.rodeoaustin.com.

Images

Tracking down usable photos for the book was an adventure. I saw many more images documenting this organization's activities and participants than could be included here. Although Austin photographer Neal Douglass took innumerable photos of the show in the 1940s and 1950s while working for the *Austin American-Statesman*, many of these are long gone. I was thrilled to find three in the Neal Douglass Collection at the Austin History Center. The History Center also had a few additional photos of the show in its collections. The Chamber of Commerce had only a handful of photos in its files, but they were the earliest originals I could find of the show. Documentary photographer Russell Lee took dozens of photos of the show in the 1950s. The iconic images included here were made available by the Dolph Briscoe Center for American History at the University of Texas at Austin. Photos appearing in the Austin dailies in the 1960s and 1970s had questionable ownership and could not be used, but the *Austin American-Statesman* provided photographs from its archives from the 1980s and 1990s. Other photographs and ephemera were made available by the Star of Texas Fair and Rodeo and by individuals.

INDEX

Star of Texas Fair and Rodeo (*cont.*)
    horse shows, 81; marketing effort,
    88–90; melding of rodeo and music,
    69–72; mission of, 1–5, 78; name
    change to, 78; professional staff
    resources, 87–89; property growth of,
    90–91; staff and volunteer structure,
    32–35; statewide expansion, 78–81;
    Western art show, 80, *81*; youth
    livestock auction changes, 81–83
steer competition, *24*, 50, *80*, 103–5
Steer Syndicate, 104
Steffens, L. D., 101
Stone, W. O., 103
Storm, Lynn, 101
Strait, George, *68*
Strange, Don, 48
Stroup, Hil, 102
supporters profile, 32–39

Talley, Shelley, 33, 57
Taylor, Brother, *66*
Team Rodeo Austin, 74
Teich, Bryan, *92*, 102
television coverage of rodeo, 72, 74, 84
Texas Draft Horse and Mule Show, 81
Texas Exposition and Heritage Center:
    construction of, 32, 39, 46–47;
    rodeo in, 67, 75; selling of to Travis
    County, 51–52; settling in to, 48–51
Texas Parks and Wildlife Department,
    29
Texas School for the Deaf, 14
Texas Sesquicentennial, 54–55
Thomas Carnival, 27, 29
ticket sales management, 87
Top Hand Award, *33*
Toyota, 104
Travis, Merle, 61
Travis County: agriculture in, 3, 6–7, 8,

56; preservation of local livestock
    show (2000–2005), 79–80; sale of
    Expo Center to, 51–52; urbaniza-
    tion of, 3, 56
Travis County Agricultural Extension
    Service, 1, 7, 8
Travis County Boys' Livestock Show, 9
Travis County Club Boys' Calf Show, 9
Travis County Commissioners Court,
    31, 37, 52
Travis County Exposition Center, 3–5,
    5, 58, 91. *See also* Texas Exposition
    and Heritage Center
Travis County Junior Livestock Show,
    13
Travis County Registered Hereford
    Breeders Association, 14
Travis County Sheriff's Posse, *55*
Travis County Youth Show, 80
Tucker, Hayden, 105
Tucker, Reagan, 104
Tuggle, Cullen, *74*
Tuggle, Shaun, 34, 74, 81–82, 89–90,
    91, 102
Turner, Travis, 104
Turrieta, Gilbert, 102

Union Stock Yards as home for live-
    stock show, 15

values, promoting hard work and
    responsibility, 3, 43, 57
Voelker, Stan, 57, 59, 60, 91, 102
volunteers, 10, 32–35, 42, 46–47, 59
Voyles, Claude, 101

Wallrath, Richard, 36, 56, 104
Walter E. Long Municipal Park, 44
Watson, Gene, 44
Wattinger, H. E., 8

Weber, Fred, 33, 80, 83, 102, 105
Weisman, John, 102
Weiss, Glenn, 103
Weiss, Jason, 56, 104
Western art show, 35, 80, *81*
Western heritage: and Go Western
    Week, 16–18; Graham Center, 38,
    91, *92*; Lamb on importance of,
    86; parade as promoter of, 54–55;
    preservation goal, 3
White, Mark, 50–51
Wieland, Roland, 103
Wiggins, Kerry, *82*, *92*, 102
wildlife exhibit, 29
Wilke, Katherine, 104
William Gammon Insurance, 104
Williams, Don (musician), 49
Williams, Donnie (president), 60, 102
Williamson County Buyers Group,
    104
Willingham, Ed, 103
Willingham, K. D., 11, 13
Witfield, Ronnie, 64
Wolman, Tee, 64
women, participation in organization,
    91–92
World War II, 10
Wroe, E. R. L., 8

Xtreme Bull Riding, *71*, 72

youth fair, 35, 42–43, 50, 79–80
youth livestock show: at 1954 show,
    18; bidders' and buyers' support
    for, 35–36; changes (2000s), 79–80,
    81–83; educational purpose, 1–3;
    retreat from larger show to, 23
youth participation in staging of show,
    13
youth video journalism contest, 81